Born In The Wrong Country

By

Milton Lee Norris

ISBN: 978-0-578-00048-0

Milton Lee Norris
135 West 96th Street
Apt. 5 E
New York, New York
10025-9221
212-865-1453
mleenor@earthlink.net
mleenor@wrongcountry.com

Table of Contents:

PART I

1. Paranoia, How To & America's Flaws   1
2. Jesus Is Not Coming Back Right Now: Take Care of Yourself!   27
3. The Brainwashing of Americanism and Religion   36
4. Forgiveness   62
5. Medical Terrorism, Modern-Day Slavery & Discrimination   67

PART II

6. Looking at Forgiveness   97
7. But You're Different   103
8. How Does One Destroy Gifts   108
9. Let Us Not Lose Focus on Saving Lives   118
10. What the Lord Has for Me, 'Nobody Can Take Away   139
   Candles and Tears   148
   Joy, Praise and Love   151
11. Rude People   161
   If It's Done Out of Love   169
12. Passion   172
13. Remembering Slavery, White Man's Cruelty, Stolen Children   191
   A Pray for the Slaves That Have Gone Before   198
   i. America's Sick Humor   201
14. Crimes the White Man Has to Answer for   203
15. Black & White in this country   207
   I Light This Candle   214

This book is dedicated in part to someone that was very special to me; he was at one time my confidant, and my companion for a short time. He was a wonderful man with a few flaws, but that's not what is important right now. I am giving him the credit that he is due. It was he who kind of inspired me and told me to write again, and it was a favorite writer he loved that I too began to read while living with him. He had a wonderful book collection which I made use of. I picked *Another Country* by the late James Baldwin, and that helped begin opening up my imagination through reading some of his books. I fell in love with James Baldwin's writing too, and after a while he seemed like an old friend, especially the more I read, but more so when I started writing.

There is of course the woman that is closest to my heart, my mother, for without her input in my life as a guiding force, I would not have reached this pinnacle. Many people think that she was that silent force, but with me she is more than that. I understood her quiet manner, her movements and her looks, so soft and gentle, yet so supreme. This is for the very special lady in my life that I simply call "Mom"; my mother and my friend, who always told me that if ever I needed anything, all I had to do was call, and if I wanted to come home, I always had one there. She always added a little more from her heart when telling you something; she would say that we might not have much, but you know we'll find something here, for this was her way that she had of comforting and soothing your every thought. It was also a way of letting you know that there was plenty at home.

There is my father, who like my mother was always a believer of education and reading. He supported me in ways that no one else did when I became the epileptic child just trying to be normal; he helped me by not really treating me any differently. Dad would always tell me not to stay in New York and starve; he told me to come home if I wanted to because at least I would have plenty to eat; he said, "You know we always have plenty to eat here."

So, Mom, Dad, this book is for you. For after all those years as two, you finally became as one, and for all the love you've given in your own special ways, and for the strength you've shown me throughout some troubling years. This book is about all of us in many ways, as it is about our heritage that was never taught in the schools where I went. This book too is dedicated to the African-American people of color, our real history that wasn't taught when I grew up in Bridgeport, Connecticut.

Since writing this book this lady whom I call my lady mom, my brown angel, passed on at the beginning of 2006. Although I miss her immensely, I am strengthened by her spirit, which continues to flow.

(AAPC stands for African-American People of Color.)

PART I

1. Paranoia, How To & America's Flaws

In times such as today, one is called on to watch and listen to everything that is going on or seems to be going on in their immediate surroundings. Nowadays, there are cautionary statements said and or heard over the loudspeakers at airports, bus terminals, train stations, and subway stations that caution everyone to keep an eye on their bags, that tell people not to hand their bag to anyone, or leave it alone for any amount of time. They also caution people that if you see anything suspicious, or if you see a bag or package that is left unattended for any length of time, to report it to the authorities or nearest law enforcement officer. And when checking in at the airports, you are asked if you left your bags unattended for any length of time, or if you handed them off for someone else to watch before checking in. Something like that is said over the loudspeakers, and to you by whoever is checking you in before boarding. Now

1

a paranoid person is probably going a little berserk right about now, and for the so-called normal people like you, you are probably on the verge of really becoming paranoid yourself. Well isn't this fun? No this is making the crazier people more crazed, and it is making you just frazzled beyond your own recognition. People are now being asked to become much more observant than in the past, things have become much more heightened, or as many would say more on edge, and when the feeling of being on edge comes over some people, a paranoid situation can occur, or simply put, you become paranoid.

Paranoia is something that can settle into those brains of yours without you really becoming aware of it. Others around you probably feel a sense of what you are feeling, maybe even greater, so you do have plenty of company, you're not in this alone, they are probably just as paranoid as you. However, you really have no way of knowing that because if there was something that you needed to ask them, such as did they perhaps notice a little something odd over there, it wouldn't really be of any help to you because number one, you're too paranoid to ask anyone anything, and number two, you don't want them to think you a little strange for asking. Or you're probably thinking that if you do ask, then they'll not only think you a little strange, but then they might think that you are the paranoid one. These intense surroundings have thrown us off guard more than we realize. How our minds play tricks us, or is it someone else that is tricking our mind? Talk about paranoid, we can't even think straight anymore.

As you try and live a so-called normal life, whatever normal living is today, you notice how tense people are, especially right after something happens because everyone is or has been affected on some level. For instance, right after the WTC on

9/11/2001 is a prime example. For me it was the jet planes, which never bothered me before. But in any case our government has really gone overboard in helping create the level of paranoia that exists today. They then tell everyone to relax, and go on about your lives are normal because they have everything under control, and that's when you really get paranoid, or at least you should, for it was the supreme arrogance of this United States of America that got us into this mess to begin with. So even though over seven years have passed since 9/11, so much of America remains in a heightened state of paranoia, especially in your larger metropolitan cities, and people are tense. Don't let the government change the colors alert, or give a new warning, which is said to be authentic, then so many of the population becomes just like static electricity – they're wired.

As we journey through life's magnificent intertwining roads, we get accustomed to changing settings as we travel, some good, some not so good, and some which are just strange or peculiar. But in this ever-changing environment that we observe today, and with all of the heightened security, we just might find that they are in fact quite peculiarly disturbing, and this doesn't please any of us; we have never felt anything like this before. What a road our lives spin out for us. At some time, we get to the point where we feel that we must make a detour or create a new path that is just for us, and we don't want anyone to follow us on that road. This time, this is your baby, and this time you don't feel like any company from anyone – not from your mother, father, brother, sister, cousin, or your best friend, whom you usually tell mostly everything, or your lover if you're fortunate enough to have one, and if you do, you'd like them to wait until you ask them to join, that's if you do. You see, it

3

doesn't matter how intense things are, this journey is somewhat of a special journey that God has decided you must travel on your own, and He'll be there to assist you.

Believing that I am being given a chance of a lifetime, and such a rare opportunity, it's a feeling that has been greatly enhanced, for it feels as if in a way I've been commissioned, and what a great feeling this is. It is my belief that I should take a journey through my mind, my heart, my soul, and my spirit and put them together to write and tell this story. This particular part of the journey is saying to write something commenting on the state of what this country is doing, has done, and is not doing. To write something about a flaw that this country has, a flaw that is ignored – you know it, you were born here, and you have been aware of this flaw for quite some time. This country is flawed; things of value usually have a flaw somewhere because like in a gem, they may be gem quality, but they are not perfect. A gem can be more highly valued because of a said flaw, because it's usually a tiny imperfection that raises its value, because it is so extremely rare. I really don't know whether this nation would qualify as gem quality or not, the flaw is far too great, the imperfection is just too wide, so this would not bring the value to a higher level, it would only serve to decrease the level. This flaw is far too great, it is an appalling flaw, and this country is terribly flawed with this great imperfection called "arrogance".

A flaw is something that is usually equated with a strange kind of mark, something a little different that sets something off from being perfect. By no means does this flaw prohibit the United States from being perfect, perfection of this government is not even a concern, as it is doesn't even come close to that kind of utopian society, an idea that would suggest such perfection would not even come close in a masquerade. Reality check – this is just one of many, for that flaw, among other things, will become apparent as we will discover while unraveling or exposing things along the way.

The things in life that one is being allowed to do, the gifts and the opportunities to utilize them, and thus share them, are what are called blessings. Believing that blessings are meant to be shared brings a sort of infuriation to mind, but that will be discussed later. One might wonder how strange it is to put the words "blessings" and "infuriation" in the same sentence, that this doesn't compute. Perhaps some would say that this does makes sense, and in fact it makes perfect sense; I can think of so many potential blessings, countless blessings that were in essence taken away from all of us, from all of the people of this country, and from another. These blessings were just snatched away, and it makes me feel like crying for all of the beloved who never even had a chance, who were suffocated by an intrusion of some kind or other by this society, this government that we live under. Then you have those that were never given a chance or opportunity, but who are alive.

The mind is a picture sponge, and the state of mind encompasses many things such as remembering, watching, observing, feeling, hearing, and sensing things that have been building inside for quite some time. You watch and you listen, you hear and you play things back in your mind to see if what you saw or heard, or what you thought you heard, was really true. Then you say to yourself, ah yes it's true, it wasn't your mind playing tricks on you, you saw what you saw and you heard exactly what you thought. What a precise instrument, and we all possess this mind, some of higher qualities than others, but like other instruments, they have keys so that different notes can be produced to create different sounds, and so that different melodies can be played.

I've known for a very long time that I am an old soul because the pain that I feel is not just of today, it's far too much and too great. Being the kind of person that can see, and in a sense feel more than I see, it's as if my mind were magnifying these things that it is sending me. My imagination runs wild, and for many years each time I closed my eyes to go to sleep, I saw faces, different faces. The real ugliness is felt, one sees a lot more when images come into view, images of things not recognized, then that sheer ugliness is felt, and at times to imagine the pain is pain that can be unbearable. It seems as if I am feeling the pain that my mother, my father, my grandparents, great-grandparents and great-great-grandparents felt. Oh that strife, what utter sickness I feel just thinking about it sometimes, what they must have gone through; and how they must have felt in such a dark, such a dirty, and in such an unfriendly time and place. Those yester years as slaves, tormented by such an uncouth society, and not having anywhere to run, or home to go to, what a way of being incarcerated. In such vast a land, but yet they were still in a jail; a prison where they were in essence working for their keep, but unlike an ordinary prisoner, they had done nothing wrong except being born Black of color and beautiful in another country thousands of miles away. This didn't make sense, and looking back on all of this doesn't bring any kind of closure to such a once immaculate people.

As time progressed, the horror didn't decrease, for a slave was a slave, meant to obey his or her master, and still they were not in control. Then as years passed quickly on, and slavery ended, still the terror remained, for they still couldn't speak their mind, the jobs that they had to accept were for much less pay than their White counterparts. Destruction, the White man destroys, and it has been said that he destroys all that he touches because he or she is envious and greedy, envious about what God gave my people. Envy can be so destructive, and once something is destroyed, it can never be the same. Being envious would have been fine, for it is a part of every man and woman, of all races and nationalities – though a flaw it's still a human characteristic. Be envious but don't destroy, be envious but don't murder, be envious but don't shoot, don't burn, be envious but don't rape, be envious but don't hang, and don't rob us, don't, but you did, and went on to do much more, more than you should ever have done.

So now let's begin by saying that today is a beautiful time, strange yet it is a time filled with mysterious wonderments, a time when music and writing plays such an important part of our lives. Writing seems to be the way to highlight these notes of importance whether it is imperfect or not, and like music both can be intriguingly enhancing. Believing that this is a significant time, and also a significant time of my life, if perhaps difficult, I seem to be heading into what feels like one of the best parts of my aging process. I seem to hear my thoughts clearer than I have for a long time. Hearing the voices, it feels as if this journey is taking on more of a can-do, must-do atmosphere than at any other time of my life. This seems like a must-do journey for I've learned how to walk, now I must learn how to run the ladders of life's structure and balance seems to be of utmost importance in the factors that matter in this climb.

As one grows older things seem to change whether they've really changed or not, but you've grown older, so maybe this is what happens, or what seems to happen. In any case, you are still here, so remember you're forging ahead. Though there are many who would rather not be part of that older generation and look at aging as an old unwanted lover, be grateful that you are still alive to continue your journey. We've all been brainwashed about our youth, how to stay young, how to feel young, and of course how we can look youthful without the wrinkles of an aging old man or woman. And yes, don't forget the sex part, we do want to be able to relive the sex of our younger days, where once was never enough, and it was so easy to keep on going sexually, and to have another climax, a second time, a third and perhaps a fourth time. What joy that brought to our hungry souls, for it was good. The plastic surgeons, pharmacists, the hairdressers, beauticians, cosmetologists and clothes manufacturers are all having a ball. If you have any investments in any of these areas, or companies that make the medicines, such as those pharmaceutical companies and other companies that manufacture vitamins, whether over-the-counter or prescriptions, then you will make a bundle. Or if you're a designer of high fashion, you'll be at the top and financially secure. And if you have investments in saunas, spas, or gyms, this too could make you financially set. Unfortunately for many of us, this means that we will continue to work at making others rich, for we are the ones that will continue to buy and continue paying out; we're the hungriest of consumers, and we're the ones who need them the most because we're aging.

Looking into this wide spectrum of things and the color wheel at play, this massive evolving revolving high-tech scheme of things that spins throughout our lives, there is something about the colors that I see which disturbs me. Things may be the same color, perhaps it is the lighting that may be off, and also what I hear now gets on my nerves more than it did when I was younger, and the smell of things really gets to me now much more than it did in the yesterdays of my emergence.

Great news, it's not me; it is this country that is making me feel this way, and do you know why? Okay, let's begin with this government, our nation. It doesn't seem as if this is really a kinder, gentler nation, not at all, and for Americans living in the United States of America, well, it seems as though our times are much more uncertain, much more chaotic, and our government doesn't seem to be in real giving mood– at least for it's citizens.

As life has me stepping forward, and hopefully marching to the right beat in the right direction, this seems like it is also a time that is beaconing me, when life starts to call out, then it's time to do different things. Right now something seems to be calling me like a wounded animal that is trapped needing help to free itself. Or like a mother that is crying out for her lost child as she begins to weep, and it's saying that it is time for me to write, and to begin with the reality that I see, of the love that I've shared, and bring forth those thoughts that have been pondering in my mind for some time, to bring them to the forefront of this journey that I am traveling. So be brave and write, what was I waiting for, the images were there, the sound was there, and the temperature was getting hotter day by day, so why wait?

Sharing is very important, not that it wasn't yesterday, it's always been important, but now it seems even more so. Time seems to be moving faster than it did a week, a month or a year ago, when before it seemed as if you had all the time in the world, now you quickly realize that you don't have nearly as much as you once had. The aging process seems to have sped up, and now you're the one that is no longer that young adult, now you're middle-aged, imagine that, they're calling you middle-aged, and it began at forty, and here you are almost sixteen years beyond that, so there is no question that you are a middle-aged person. The dictionaries and the information on the

Internet agree, stating that when a person reaches the ages between forty and sixty, that person is considered middle-aged, some go as far as stretching it to end at sixty-four or sixty-five, but there is no question about where you are. Now it doesn't seem as if you have all the time left in the world anymore, you think of sharing even more because now things seem even more precious than they once did, and that seems as if it were only yesterday, but yesterday is gone forever, and it's not coming back.

It's not like I wasn't taught to share, exactly the opposite, we were taught to share, but as one reaches different pinnacles of life, it is now even more important to reach out to people, and in a different way. It becomes easier to talk about things that you would have never discussed, but that too comes with age. The needs of people seem to be of greater importance, your own needs have expanded, and the needs of this society is what is being stressed today, and those needs are beginning to stress people out. But whether they're being met, now that all depends on whom you're talking to, the proletariat or the governmental hierarchy. Well, we know that the proletariat in any society is the one that suffers, so it would be wise to listen to them – they're nearly always the people in need.

Today, writing seems to be the exact tool that I need to express what it is that I want to convey, tomorrow it might be painting, for pictures have always fascinated me, or photography, which is already a hobby of mine, or perhaps sculpture, to be able to mold something from the mind that God gave you, using your hands and fingertips to shape something out of clay or bronze, or wood, and then who knows, perhaps drawing or singing or a combination of different tools. Like I said, it doesn't seem as if I have all the time in the world anymore. I am open, but right now I'm listening to this voice within me, it is the voice of precision, for it is the spirit that is instructing me, and today it is telling me to write; therefore, I must follow the instruction of the teacher. Believing in that higher power, I listen, this is what I'm being led to do, and in this case I'm being told to write.

One has to care about things in order to really proceed in life. Caring takes up such a vast amount of time in our lives, so whether people say they do or not, most people do care about something. Whether they choose to display it or not is up to them. Perhaps they're too shy to let things out for fear of what others might think or say, those are some of the pressures that society has created. There is that caring can make you laugh, cry or it can make you very angry, things are either getting on your nerves or it's like you're watching a comedy. For me, it's things that are getting on my nerves, comedy makes one laugh, the events of today and many of those of the past don't make me laugh, they make me want to cry, and some incidents do make me cry. Some of us are more sensitive than others, and I admit that it doesn't take much for me to cry, and I don't feel ashamed that tears will stream down my face – I was born that way. Injustices make me cry, watching what people do to one another in so many negative ways can make me cry – destruction, stealing, lying, cheating, distrusting, hurting, demeaning, and the list goes on.

Like I said, the noises and colors are different, or it may be that I'm getting a little older and things, people…oh yeah, their stupidity really gets on my nerves now more than in my yesterdays. You might say that it's all about growing up, and that would probably be partially correct because today it is more frightening than my yesterdays. Before there wasn't as many ways to steal from people, there weren't any computers, there was no Internet, and there definitely wasn't as many ways to annihilate people. Today we're living in a much more savvy and hi-tech environment – air travel, high-speed railways, high-speed cars, everything is faster and it's much more dangerous. I hear screeches now that really do me in, years ago that was more bearable, but not today. Explosions seemed like an ordinary noise in the a big city, you know when you heard a car backfire, and hearing the sound jets coming in closer than usual didn't make me want to jump out of my skin, now they do, now they really bother me. Now when I hear the sound of a jet very close to me in this city I almost freeze, and this is not a coincidence, it's not just about me getting older, though I know that plays some part. I know the real reason, it's because of 9/11; my nerves just aren't the same anymore.

Today my heart is forced to beat to the rhythm of a different drummer. Some of this is fine for life is ever-changing, this I know, and this I understand, but some of this I can really do without. In fact, if it were up to me, I would…well; it doesn't matter because right now the choice is not mine. Yes things now are really beginning to get on my nerves.

I'm a caring person, but sometimes I guess I really don't want to care, but it is in my nature, and when I see things, accidents, violence, crimes, crimes involving children, terrible crimes that cause so much death and destructions, I pray. You might ask, "Is that all you do?" My answer to you would be that this is what I can do with grace, and whether you agree or not, someone needs to pray, so be happy that there are those of us who do pray, and also this is what I can afford to do. I don't think I've prayed this much since my landlord changed, Clinton left the White House, and 9/11, and the other one had to be selected by the Supreme Court. To me that was and is a real reason and need for prayer because to put it bluntly this man in the White House has pissed off the entire world. People from all over the world cannot stand him, but now they are feeling the same toward you and me – we live in this country, so we've become a target of that hate. I've never sworn as much as I do now, and I wasn't raised that way, so I won't give you an example, let's just say that I too get really pissed off. I wonder, can that too be attributed to the aging process, or is that all to do with the culmination of events of our times? You be the judge.

When it comes to caring, sometimes I wonder who really cares. It's a word so often misused that I feel that it's almost akin to being lost. It's the same as when someone tells you they love you after they have mistreated you, abused you, and then promised to do the right thing. You look at them wanting to believe them because you do love them, and then they say it again, this time sounding a little more sincere and convincing. Again you look at them, but this time you make eye-to-eye contact, and as they begin to say how much they love you, you put up a hand that says stop, then you utter a few words to them, "Show me or get out."

Caring is like love in many ways, they both have to be shown. Anyone who has ever had a loving relationship knows that love has to be shown, well, so does caring and before one can do either, first they must know what love is, what caring is, and then they must know how to do it. You must know how to love, and you must know how to care for someone or something. So many of us just don't get the how-to part in life. In order to know how to do something, you must first realize that these simple words involve something greater, and that takes effort. Reality has to strike your mind before you'll ever find out how to do anything.

When one makes an effort, it means that you are saying to the other person that you will be responsible, and that's the key – responsibility. Responsibility is something people often get confused about because it means that they must put part of themselves and/or their reputations on the line, so many people aren't quite ready to expose themselves that way; taking off their clothes would be more their style. You see just as when they're exposing their bodies, they also know that this means that someone will be judging them, someone will be taking a critical look at them, and unlike their body, they might not be as confident, and they know that they will not be able to hide their real self any longer. So whether they're confident or whether they don't want you to see all of them, now their words and actions will show exactly what they're about, there is no escaping the facts this time. There are many of us who don't want to put ourselves on the line for anything, but if you're going to be responsible, that is exactly what you must to be willing to do.

You thought it was simple to love and simple to care, didn't you? For instance, caring and loving parents have already made a decision to take the responsibility to care for, to love, and to nurture their children; they know that this is a very serious responsibility. Now there are those parents that are totally clueless because they had no idea what is involved, or they would have never decided to leave their child on the church steps, or much worse to put their child in the garbage. These individual didn't really know anything about love, caring, or responsibility. They were just as clueless because they had no idea of what was involved, they hadn't thought about the responsibilities of how to care for this special gift, this little person, or what finances were needed to clothe, feed, and house this special one, or even what headaches there might be involved in raising a child.

So you see one needs to be responsible. You see there is a 'how to' do many things that we do, things we do every day but take for granted. There is how to eat, there is a proper way, how to wash your hands before leaving the bathroom, how to say hello to your neighbor or someone that you don't really know, how to make them feel welcome and comfortable. How to buy something, how to own something, how to rent something, how to be happy, how to sell something, how to educate yourself, how to read, how to grow, how to heal, how to breathe, how to talk to someone, how to take care of yourself mentally and physically, how to get dressed, how to undress, how to have sex, how to study, how to exercise, how to write, how to speak, how to shop, how to drive, how to park, how to swim, how to run, how to say excuse me and how to say thank you, how to use a computer, how to search the Internet, how to shut down your PC, and the list goes on and on. You see without the how to, so many things sound simpler than they really are, that is until you start to do some of them. It is all a learning process, caring and loving is not just done, it's not that simple, one may think it works that way, but it doesn't. Take relationships that fall apart because the love is not what someone thought it was, perhaps they didn't really discuss how they wanted to be loved, or what was expected in this love relationship – that does happen sometimes. There is a how to love somebody, believe me, and there is how to be a friend! What you are willing to do is often involved in a love relationship. When you really begin to think about what is involved, you begin to realize that it takes a little knowledge of these two words, what they really mean, not just to you but to the other person, then once you begin to realize that, you really begin to understand that you do need to know how to do just about everything in life.

People are fascinating characters, and my belief is that manners tell a lot about a people or a person, as does respect for oneself, so hold that thought. When someone says they care about you, it also involves tone, again the how to comes into play, how are they saying that they care for you? This is really a need-to-know thing that people need to pay attention to because it's all a reflection on who you are. And speaking about the tone of caring in this country, simply put, it sucks.

We don't have national healthcare, all of our children don't have the books they need for school, and some don't have the right classroom, or even a classroom, yet you hear city, state and government officials say that they care. People don't have jobs, yet this country is outsourcing jobs to other countries at an alarming rate. Perhaps the United States of America is moving, and it's just that they forgot to inform its people. People are homeless, diseases are running rampant, people need clothing, people need food, people need housing, people need medicine, and they need all of these things right here in this country, we don't need them overseas. Well over two hundred billion dollars has been spent on this Iraqi war by this current administration, and they say they can't afford to give you healthcare, and that the government needs to cut back. Why can't they cut back on the spending in the countries they are destroying and spend our money here at home where it belongs, where the people are, the people that they keep saying they care about, the tax-paying people like you and me? Better still, why don't they just stop with these wars altogether, then there wouldn't be any need to spend billions of dollars trying to rebuild a country that they spent billions of dollars destroying?

You see I really don't like the colors that I'm seeing today, it's very simple, and it's plain to see that this government doesn't care, they just don't care, they don't give a damn about you or me. Drugs are still coming into this country, especially into the poorer neighborhoods, dealers are making thousands, and your real dealers are making millions, but the government continues to allow a steady stream of drugs into this country. To hear them talk, these are the ones that they say fell through the cracks, and then they say that nothing is perfect, well why not? When they want to make a perfect launch into space, going millions or billions of miles into outer space, or hookup with another spacecraft already out there, they do it, and they do it with perfection because that is what is required, and they know it, so why can't we expect perfection when it comes to keeping America's poor off of drugs? Doesn't America's poor deserve this perfection, aren't America's children worth more than a spacecraft going into outer space? If this country can do all that and more, why can't they stop the drugs and guns from coming in through these so-called cracks, or are they being allowed to infiltrate this country on purpose? One must ask these questions, especially when they speak of the perfection that they want from the people, like paying their taxes so that you can do all of those things.

It's always interesting how this government can do so many things that they want to do, and while they're cutting back on things that their own people need, they can always find millions or billions of dollars to do what they want, that never fails. And they can usually give themselves a pay hike at will, that's always been a bone of contention, but they are being allowed to treat the American people unfairly, so you must ask why, but be willing to answer the question, that's right, just think about it.

These drugs are layering the poorest of the poor communities, while they are spending billions elsewhere in other countries, and on satellites that continue to travel to Mars and Jupiter, and some crash or are lost for that matter, but even more money is found from someplace. Then they will continue to spend more billions as they continue to try to find more planets, more stars, and other galaxies, so where is this money that they don't supposedly have coming from?

When it come to programs for the people of this country, then they truly won't have the money, that magical genie who has found money for everything else will have disappeared, and now you'll be told that they have to cut back. The job cutback is easy, Americans should know how some of those jobs were cut because your country just outsourced them to overseas, the food they are giving to folks overseas too, and the healthcare programs is probably being given to the Iraqi people with the amount of money that this country is spending over there. We know that they have to rebuild Iraq and Afghanistan because they spent billions destroying them, so the money for your housing programs is probably being spent overseas, as is your children's education for their education, so in a nutshell, with all of this money gone and going overseas, this government must be moving. So when someone asks where America's money has gone, don't shrug your shoulders like you don't know, just tell them that it's gone overseas, that you gave it away. And where is the program of America's common sense, well if there was one, that too must have gone overseas, trailing the money. A caring nation or a caring government wouldn't treat people like this country treats its people. But guess what, this government can always find many ways of spending your money when it comes to helping out other countries, those are the people and the governments they wish to help. They've become the philanthropist or the Auntie Mame government of the world, that is except for this country.

You see there is a different color to words today, there is a greater artificiality, the words still mean the same thing, but we've colored them differently, some might call it rhetoric, but whatever it is, the human spirit is lacking. The meaning seems to have changed, but that's not it, it's the people that lack sincerity, and if you lack sincerity, then you really can't call yourself a caring person, or a caring nation. If you don't believe what is being said, look up the word "caring", and then look up the word "sincerity". There is a spirit involved in so many things; my belief says that the human spirit is lacking in this country.

What's happening in this country has aggravated me so much that my mind, body, and spirit feel as if something is gnawing at them purposely, and now those feelings are like those of ripened peaches ready for consumption, but it's not a sweet smell, it's sour; it's like something that is spoiling or has spoiled. What a state for anyone, and to feel this way about the country where they were born, raised, and live is even more devastating – it's rotten, and what a feeling.

As my thoughts are filling up with anxiety, as the colors seem to take on a different light, and as the smell is that of something wasting away, I pray that I will be able to continue seeing beauty, and I also pray that my life will continue teaching me without transforming me into a different person who is unable to focus, to see or hear those wonderful sounds of nature. As frustrating as this government has made things, I don't want to become cynical because life is beautiful, and there are many beautiful people in our world, and in our country, and I definitely don't want to become arrogant, so I pray that this frustration won't have an effect that would cause this kind of change. Arrogance is not a friend of mine; to me it is almost the equivalent of someone showing their ass to you in public, for that would be a vulgar display, and I don't think anyone really wants to see that. I certainly don't because not only is it a rude and crude way to communicate, in so many cases, it's not a pretty sight to look at all, and this is something that I don't find appeasing either. It is such an unsophisticated and crude way of communicating, and one should be better educated than to show their arrogance to another human being.

Arrogance is also destructive, and it is that kind of destruction that is destroying this country. You won't have any trouble spotting arrogance, it's so easily recognized in some of the people in this country, and if you have trouble locating it, for a closer look, check inside the White House, then look at your other government, city and state officials, who also appear too condescending.

There is too much fire in the world today, and now this country has added more fuel to an already hot situation by their remarks about axis of evil and a preemptive strike on Iraq. You see that flaw jumps out again; it's almost like slapping someone, they are the kind of remarks that other countries don't like, remarks that if made by another country to the USA would not be taken well at all, but this arrogant president doesn't seem to care what anyone thinks, and that can be very dangerous. Why ruffle feathers unnecessarily? This country just doesn't know how to mind its own business and deal with pertinent affairs here at home. Everywhere you look there is a hot spot, somewhere something is almost to the point of blowing up.

In the election of 2000, things in this country truly got way out of hand, so much so that things got really crazy and real ugly. The ugly American was back in business, not that he'd gone anywhere, he just resurfaced in a big and bold way, and against my people, the African-American People of Color, other people of color, and minorities. The election was being fixed right before our eyes, and it was being swept under the rug so to speak. Yet it was so blatant that too much confusion was caused, thus causing damage that could not be undone, and safeguards were in place which forced the Supreme Court to step in, then favors that were owed were simply called in.

People were getting ready to finally go to sleep when it was announced that Gore had won Florida, but then something happened that I don't think ever happened in a national election before. All of a sudden there was another announcement not too soon after saying sorry, that they had to recant what they had said, now it no longer seemed that Gore had taken Florida, and then people knew that something had happened; Black people definitely knew what was up. Later it was learned that some people had not been allowed to vote, there was a high degree of voter tampering, and some votes were simply deleted. So who was not being allowed to vote? It was the Black people that weren't being allowed to vote, the AAPC, and some other democratic voters as well, but it was primarily the Black vote, and those that were deleted were democratic votes that had been cast. After all of this mayhem, and rather than go through the painful ordeal and do the honest and correct thing and recount all of the votes and let people vote again, the higher-ups in this land said no, and that's when the Supreme Court stepped in to select your president, and that's also when the entire world laughed at the United States of America – again.

Before this figure came into power, many people were heard commenting that they didn't trust this man at all, and my opinion was that it seemed to me that he wanted a war. Have you ever just had a bad feeling about something or someone, when you knew that something wasn't right? Well, this was the same feeling that I had about this man; I felt that something just didn't jell, and this feeling just wouldn't go away, it only intensified! This was one of those times that, unfortunately, my feelings turned out to be right on the money, low and behold, that's what he got us into after 9/11, and after getting the Patriot Bill passed.

No one really knew what was going on, but in haste and panic, so it would seem, our senators and congressmen and women signed a bill that they had not even read. Would you sign papers concerning your money or your property without first reading them? Would you sign a note for a house payment without reading it? Would you sign for your child to attend a school without reading or without understanding what would be required of you for your child to attend this school, and how much money it would cost you? I don't think so. But our senators, congressmen and women signed that extremely important bill that became law without first reading it, that is all except one.

This is your government, and if you allow them to treat you one way and then complain about it afterwards, then you have let them sign away your rights. And then if you don't do anything about it, God help you. Well, God help us because in essence that's what happened when our elected officials signed that bill, in effect, they screwed all of us.

Those who think that this was just a coincidence or accidental aren't really thinking. What we had in the White House up until then was only a figure, a sad figure at best, but a figure facsimile of what an American president was supposed to be. The Supreme Court put him there; the American people did not, but they would do their best to groom him. He was even laughable, but very dangerous mind you, now he was being given even more power, and history would soon repeat itself purposely four years later, only this time he would have a greater number of the American people voting for him in the popular vote. However, many still believe that the election of 2004 was stolen in much the same way that it had in 2000, so it too was a crooked election.

Sometime afterward, when introducing Bill Clinton, a congressman was heard saying: "It gives me great pleasure to introduce the last elected president of the United States of America." People laughed, but as sad as this statement was, he was telling the truth.

Things happen or are forced to happen for a reason, my belief being, so that they could take more control of the world, so that they could dominate and be the controlling factor in the entire world. This is something they truly wanted, they didn't listen to the American people, they refused to listen to the UN, and they refused to listen to most of their former allies. They just ignored what the world consensus was telling them, those millions of people worldwide that demonstrated in the streets, that were yelling and screaming, saying no war, telling America not to invade Iraq. The American people didn't matter; the Republicans had fixed the vote, taken power, so here they were acting like the dictators they had once shunned, or was this just a ploy? But they told you that they cared, and were doing this for the American people too.

It has been said that top influential families, the real moneymakers, are the ones that really control our society and this country. This country has many extremely wealthy citizens who can be like spoiled children, many of them spoiled rotten by their wealthy parents and grandparents, who think that the American dollar can buy them anything their heart desires, even with the shrinking American dollar, but they don't have to worry about that because they're heavily invested in the euro overseas. What a pity, a pity for those of us that live in this country, and more so a pity for Black people, whose ancestors were brought over to this country hundreds of years ago as slaves, that were bought and stolen by White men from this country, your forefathers. Though today there are Blacks that are extremely rich in this country, make no mistake, whether you have been spoiled like your White counterparts, and though you contribute a vast amount of knowledge and wealth in this country, don't ever believe that this country holds you up as an equal to the White families. How America thinks of you is exactly how America sees you.

Remember what this country does best; it participates in something that is called a "selective memory program". While listening to talks with an elderly Afro-American gentleman, and the problems that face this country concerning race and the African-American People of Color, it was said that when it came to memory of certain things, the United States of America seemed to be forgetful, that they had a kind of amnesia, historical amnesia, and the gentleman called this country the "United States of Amnesia". Blacks know all too well what a convenient memory this country has when it pertains to people of color. The rest of you will soon find out that what we know holds true for you too, especially when the time comes for them to save face. If you're a poor person or a poor family, you might begin to wonder what color you are because now if you don't have money, well you're treated just like the African-American People of Color are being treated in many ways because the bottom line is that you are poor, and this country no longer seems to give the benefit of the doubt to those who are poor, even if you are White people.

The Black race has been used by this country for hundreds of years, and believe it or not we are still being used by the Whites. That old saying that the more things change, the more they remain the same is true. Though many things have changed, and are still changing, as we look at how history is repeating itself, it is becoming more evident every day. Today jealousy plays an integral part because many Blacks are making the same amount of money as their White counterparts, and many are making more, that in itself is in a financial statement, thus enabling us to afford the same luxuries as Whites, and some of us even at a higher standard. Blacks can afford to travel and really see this world in style; we can also build and finance other Blacks and Whites. In years gone by, this was unheard of, and some of the prejudices that people hold in this country want things to revert back to the way they were, like when they were the only ones that had the financial power to do what some Blacks are now doing quite successfully.

You see when jealousy comes into play, it brings that old dog out of the barn, and when he comes out again he barks and begins to show his ugly self, and perhaps even uglier than before, now he wants to bite somebody. All of a sudden you begin to notice that more fires are starting up again, bombings of yesteryears are returning to highlight our news. And it's not just the bombings in other countries, it's a reminder of those crosses of the 1950s and 60s that are beginning to reappear, lighting up our lawns, and it isn't Jesus that is coming back either, so what's really changed?

Again we Blacks are being terrorized, but the media won't give that the airtime it gives the so-called terrorists that they try to make us believe exist predominantly outside the United States. Outsourcing, could that be possible, could they have outsourced the terrorists? This country has been the source of terrorism since around the time of the landing at Plymouth Rock. When the police are still shooting Black men, and racial profiling is running rampant, I ask you what has changed? The prison system still remains overcrowded with innocent Blacks, and some waiting on death row for a murder they never committed, and some should not even be in jail, so you tell me what's changed? When mistaken identity is always making a mistake when it comes to crime in this country and pinning the crime on the Blacks and minorities, tell me what has really changed? When the news media is always giving a qualifier identifying a Black person involved in certain crimes, but when it's not a Black person or other person of color, they don't use this qualifier, and we don't know what race this person is. For instance, you will usually hear, "The man identified was a Black male," but when it's a White male, the public doesn't hear that statement nearly as much as when it is the Black male who is alleged to have committed some crime.

So now you want me to believe that so much has changed, well just like the "how to" and the "show me" part that was spoken about earlier, well the same holds true here, show me how it has changed and make a believer out of me.

The following should be read in a rhythmic sermon-like tone, that of a Black minister in the Baptist or Methodist Church.

2. Jesus Is Not Coming Back Right Now – Take Care Of Yourself!

Contrary to what you think, Jesus is not coming back right now. I know that the Bible says He's coming back again, they say that you won't know the day or the hour, but as I keep telling folks, God did not write the Bible, man did – a White man at that; the same as the one sending all of your hard-earned money overseas, and the same that invented the typewriter – he's a jack-of-all-trades. So let's try and be very reasonable, let's try and use the logic at hand, and let's try to understand, that Jesus suffered enough, and not only did He suffer, He suffered immensely, and did so at the hands of human beings like you. So ask yourself, if you were Him, would you come back after the way that you were treated, and after what the human race did to Him the first time, tell me, would you come back? No pun intended, but I myself wouldn't be dying to come back.

We must learn to take care of ourselves; we know how to go to the doctors, so we know we had better go. Today you can see a doctor for just about anything that ails you, you can see your physicians when you need medical help, be it physical or mental help for that matter, for there's help out there, and if you can pay for it, there's even more help for you. There will not be any cures or those miracle cures from Jesus today, no friends, for He's not coming back right now. So, my friends, now that you see that Jesus is not coming back, you must be in kind of a tizzy. Well, you must think that He enjoyed the treatment that you gave Him the last time around, being treated like an ordinary Black man, you must think that He enjoyed being spit in His face by you, being nailed to a cross that you even made Him carry, being beaten before thousands of people, those spectators that looked at Him as if He were some kind of wild animal, or a dog, or as if He were a common thief, and not the peacemaker or teacher that He was, and looked at Him with their despicable faces in great disdain. You must think that He must be like you, someone who loves sadomasochistic treatment, someone who loves it when you put different holes over in their bodies. Well, He didn't care for that one at all, not at all, He thought that His Father gave you enough holes and the right functions for which to use those holes, He had no idea how warped and sick your minds were, not even when His Father tried to tell Him.

Now just imagine the Father talking to His son, Jesus, who really thought that His Father knew all about you poor, sick and depraved people, but when He got back home, and when He asked His Father if He knew, His Father looked at Him as He answered, saying; "Son I told you, and I even warned you before I sent you that what you would see and experience would blow your mind, and I also told that you had to become a real human being if the journey was to be successful. That's why you had to become human like them, so you could feel what they were feeling, so you could feel the pain, the misery, the anxiety, the frustration, the terror that these humans were feeling, and so you could experience firsthand what they were doing to each other. But remember that you told me, 'Oh Father, it really can't be all that bad,' and then I warned you again, and I said 'Son I love you,' and even though they need someone to save them, I also asked you, I asked, 'Are you sure that you want me to send you, Son, for I do love you, but if you choose to go, I will send you, but you must be absolutely sure because there is no turning back, you must go there, live and grow up there, and work there.' And, Son, I told you that this would be your decision, I told you that I'd only assist you in going, but if you should decide to go, that the journey would be a journey of no return, not until the journey was completed would you be able to return home. Then I said, 'So tell me, Son, tell me, do you really want to go? Tell me.' I said 'Think about it, you don't have to answer me now, but think and then tell me, do you really want to go or would you rather that I choose someone else, for there is still time?' You thought momentarily, then you said, 'No, Father, I don't need time to think about it, send me; it can't be that bad, for you created this earth, you created those people so it can't be that bad.'"

The Father paused and then said, "'Son, I know, but something strange happened to those people, call it greed, disobedience, arrogance, stupidity, or all of the above, but, Son, something happened to those people. If you want that I send someone else, I will because there is no turning back, but believe me when I tell you it is that bad, it's even a bit worse.' But you told me, 'Don't worry, Father, I'm not afraid.' You told me, 'Father I will be all right, send me, send me, Father.' After all of our conversation, I said, 'Oh well, Son, then I will send you.'" Now what a gift extraordinaire Jesus became.

But can you imagine how much His Father would have to

persuade Him to come back because humankind messed it all up again? Humans, who just couldn't get enough of feeling as if they were the real king and the superior being or the most intelligent. Can you imagine that? He'd probably be telling His Father, "Oh no not again, before you warned me, and I didn't listen, and I didn't have any idea. I became like those humans. I didn't realize before going that it was me who was a little like those humans before leaving you the last time because here I was telling you that it couldn't be that bad. I told you, who created those people, that it couldn't be that bad, and you told me that it might be a little worse and it was, but I told you that I really didn't need the time to think, I said send me, send me Father! But no not today, not for those idiots, those selfish people, those arrogant, pompous, condescending people, those hysterical hypocritical people, those stupid, dumb, ignorant people that only think of themselves. Oh please, Father, not for them again, no not for them please, please I beg of you, send someone else. Send someone that is more like them, and who can play their sick games and torture each other. Father, I truly am not into that. Don't you think that it would be better, even wiser, if you sent someone else more like them this time, someone more deserving, don't you? There's someone that's just dying for the chance, that is as even more boastful, more arrogant, just as rude or even ruder, but surely even nastier then they are."

Then His Father looked at his Son and asked, "Son who do you think that I should send? Tell me for you know that I value your opinion, so whom shall I send?"

And Jesus answered, saying that there was someone down there, way down there who was just like them, so send him. "He wanted to be just like you, you remember, so send him, and give him the chance to redeem himself a little bit."

Then His Father said, "Oh no, Son, you don't want me to send him, why he's a bigger snake in the grass, a bigger scoundrel, a bigger rapist, even a bigger liar, a bigger thief and bigger murderer than even them, why that would be too cruel, beyond cruel."

Then the Son said to his Father, "Listen, I went for you the last time, I'm your son, and you told me that you loved me, so send him. And perhaps this time they will learn, perhaps this time they will learn how to treat people, no matter what their color, no matter what their sex, and no matter what their sexual orientation is, so send him. Perhaps then they will learn how to become a more loving people, learn how to become a caring people, how to become a more humble people, how to become a more peaceful people, how to obey, and how to treat each other with respect. And oh, that country, that country now called the United States of America, maybe then they would finally be able to tell the whole truth about the slavery, be able tell that it was a wrong, that it was truly unjust and cruel treatment and that it was one of the greatest crimes against humanity, oh Father send him."

"Son, if that's what it takes, I think that you're right. Yes someone has to teach these arrogant people in that country a lesson. They must be shown that they don't and cannot rule My world, and they must be shown that even they must answer to someone, so yes I will send him, I will send Satan. He will know just how to lie, how to cheat, how to steal, how to burn, how to hate, how to despise, how to rape, and how to murder. And you're absolutely right, I will send him to that country that is called the United States of America/Amnesia, and let them try to outdo him, they'll not be able to hold a candle to him. He will show them how, he will show them how to, and they will learn, they will repent for then they will see how it feels when the shoe is truly on the other foot. They will become kind, they will become the gentler and warmer people that I created, they will truly know how to care for each other, how to respect each other, and how to love one another. Son, this time they will understand what you told them before leaving them to return home, they will understand, they will truly understand, how, how, how to love one another as You have loved them. I will send him, and they will learn the how to be part of life, they will learn the how to be part of caring, they will learn the how to be part of loving, and they will learn the how to be part of the life that I gave to them to share. Oh I will send him, and yes, they will learn the how to be part of everything in life, of everything that is in the life that I have given them, I will send him, and they will learn."

So you see, He wants you and me to do things for ourselves, He gave us a brain so let us begin by using it, He gave us a mind, so let's use that too, He gave us the capacity for common sense, so let's try and use that too. You should be able to use anything that doesn't require the heart, and be able use and understand it, and do a pretty good job in doing so. I said that doesn't require the heart for a reason, because so many of you are a cold, calculating, heartless people, and so many of you run this government. That is a very sad statement, but it's true, otherwise you wouldn't treat your fellow human beings the way you treat them, Black or White or any other of the ethnicities that live here, or anywhere else for that matter.

This country definitely doesn't know the meaning of a heart, not the internal organ that keeps us breathing that you've found out how to operate on at will. You've done pretty well with the mechanics of how to fix that one, why you've been transplanting that one for years, and you even know how to take it out and replace it with a high-tech artificial one that will last for some time. But there is the spiritual one, the real heart that keeps us alive, one that beats to the rhythm of another drummer, the drummer that created you, thus enabling us to do things like create, feel, care and share with your fellow people, but unfortunately that's the one you seem to have the most trouble with, otherwise you wouldn't treat your fellow humans the way that you do.

You seem to have forgotten the mechanics of the how to use this spiritual instrument, this spiritual tool, that God gave you, and there is probably a reason. The reason being that there are no mechanics involved with this heart, no, this is a heart of things that are unseen but sensed and felt. This requires that you open up yourself to give to your fellow man, so there is no mechanics involved, what must be understood is how to be a good person. You know right from wrong, everyone knows that, so it's your choice in choosing that which is right, and if you do choose that which is right, then utilizing this spiritual heart will get easier and easier every time. You see when you make the right decision in looking after your people, then this country wouldn't allow one to be so disrespectful to one another, neither would it be so disrespectful to it's own people that depend on them. If it had a heart, this country wouldn't allow a murderer to murder the minorities the way it does, and continue to get away with those murders over and over again, and it wouldn't keep allowing destruction of property to continue if it really had a heart. This government of the United States of America wouldn't allow so much pain and suffering, so much homelessness, so much starvation, so much abuse of its people, and so much disease if it really had a heart. You see disease keeps growing, it's an infestation of sorts, and some of these infestations grow faster than others, and some are growing more rapidly than others because this country hasn't put the money there to slow down this infestation because it simply doesn't have a heart. Or if they do, it's been transplanted while helping others that don't even live here. You probably thought that I was kidding before when I said perhaps the United States of America is moving, and that they forgot to inform its people, but has our country really moved, and have they forgotten to tell us about it?

Talking about transplanting and the transplanting of the heart is a very interesting subject, and it is very interesting how this government follows transplants, especially the last major one. You see a transplant is something that definitely needs a lot of follow up and care, for there are infections that can settle in and begin to destroy what has just been successfully transplanted. They can't have that, so they will follow that because they must be where their money is to monitor exactly how it's being spent, and make sure that there is no infection from another source. Oh here they make like a very concerned doctor who is checking up on their patients, and I guess they are in a sense very concerned because it's about money; in fact it's about your money that was used, and is being used. You see, for all practical purposes your government is really in Iraq now, not here, there's too much money that they've transplanted there for them to take their eyes off. It would be very irresponsible just to leave the transplant without the proper care, without actually being there, so you see, they must stay and at least monitor that transplant. So when you want to know where the real government of the United States of America is, follow where they sent the money, follow those transplants, that money trail, and it will lead you to where someone or something is all the time, and it will likely be a very hot issue.

3. The Brainwashing of Americanism and Religion

It has been said that big brother is watching us, that he is listening to what we say and to what we are doing. Well, like being terrorized, this too is nothing new for the African-American People of Color, and if you want to know how we know, well we too, we had to keep our eyes on you during slavery when you were such a unwanted and dominant force in our lives. And since then we've never taken our eyes off of you, we can't afford to. We know you all too well, you're liars and thieves of the worst kind, you even stole people; you stole our children. Look at the sons and daughters that you took away from their mothers and fathers, and from their families. Then there are treasures of various sorts that were taken when you robbed this land, and just about anything that didn't or doesn't belong to you, and we have never met any bigger liars in our time; perhaps there were many who have tried, but none have succeeded you, and that's nothing to be proud of.

You tell us that you've changed, but too much has not changed, and as they say, a leopard doesn't change his spots – this still holds true. Like Malcolm said when he reminded us of the blue-eyed devil, our enemy against the Black people. This is something that he knew, and part of this knowledge came from our history of being held in bondage by the White man. We all knew this, but like some things, perhaps we too needed to be reminded, for there are those still out to trick whomever they can, and they are quite clever, so it never hurts to have someone of your own kind to remind you before you make a mistake that might prove costly. Remember there was the Underground Railroad; we all weren't left in the dark.

This country is set on a course of intrusion and has been set on enforcing their intrusion at will; now forcing Americanism on others. When they took the African people from Africa, calling them barbaric and incarcerating them in chains, they used them as slaves because so they believed that they were lower than them, that we weren't a whole person like them, or equal to them. My, what a sick mentality. Here they came from England where they were ruled by a king and queen, a country where they were considered the subservient ones, and now they wanted to be kings and queens over someone else, but they wanted them in chains so that they could beat the savageness out of them. And because these people were a strong people, they put them in chains so that they could control them; one doesn't need to chain people that are weak. But they put them in chains too so that these beautiful people wouldn't beat the crap out of them, and so that they could pound Christianity into their brains and make them forget about their Gods, Gods they called "pagan". Now who is more barbaric than someone who chains, beats, and tortures people who have done no wrong? You historians that are out there, tell me.

You came from a country where you were tired of following the instructions from the hierarchy, where you had to be more like they wanted than you wanted to be, where you had to worship in the same fashion, and now you were creating the same thing here, but in a land that you stole from the American Indians. Tell me, with all of your fighting, and with all of your thievery, how did you ever figure that these people were barbaric and that their religion was pagan, but not you? You know you must have been smoking grass back then or some other strange weed, or perhaps you were sniffing some kind of glue, if they had any such thing back then, because it is truly mind boggling how anyone could think such a thing and continue thinking that they were the smart people. You would like me to believe that you were the sparkling Christian saviors, as shown by some of your acts displayed in the way you treated people. But you see there is a big problem because for me to even imagine how you could call anyone barbaric or their religion pagan after the way you have acted, and still act at times, would be asking me to be as crazy and as senseless as you, and that's impossible. In short, you're more than shameless, you really are disgraceful.

Then on top of that mischaracterization, you called and still call yourselves Christians, saying that you were going to teach Christianity to these barbaric people you enslaved. You really must have been on some kind of hallucinogenic drug, and you must still be if you want the rest of the world to believe such a story, such a vehement lie.

You did not even speak their language, so you could not understand them, so whatever religion they had was theirs, but you decided it was wrong. Almighty White man sitting on an imaginary throne, who in the world gave you the right, the unmitigated gall to disavow their religion? Did God come down and tell you that they were barbaric, and that their religion was pagan? I really don't think He did. With all the religions in the world, as varied and as different as they and people are, perhaps that is God's way of revealing Himself or Herself to the people.

One thing about this country that seems to never change: it is always trying to tell everyone else how they should run their government, and how they should live, basically saying that others must be wrong and the United States of America must be right. My, my, why didn't your forefathers just have the decency to be honest and say that they were coming to this new world to start a new government rather than that insipid hoax that they were coming here so they could enjoy some kind of religious freedom? People admire the truth. If that is not the most dictatorial way of thinking, then I don't know what is. America then and the United States of America today remain the same, still trying to push Americanism down everyone's throat, and it's just not in this country, look no further than Iraq right now. America must be the brainwashers of the world. As pointed out by the late Reverend Dr. Martin Luther King Jr. who once said: "God is telling America, you're too arrogant…" and I wholeheartedly agree, but I also think that Martin was really telling America to mind its own business.

To keep brainwashing Americanism all over the world the way that this country has, especially under this current administration, and under false guises has not made this country very popular at all; in fact, it has made us very unpopular. Where once we were loved by so many, now other countries are really taking a second, and third look, and when it comes to our national elections, they are laughing at us. But yet America is still going out overseas and telling others how to hold their elections, even after their own debacles, and that's putting it mildly. America is not showing itself to be a smart fellow at all these days, and at some point its arrogance has got to stop because this country is looking as if it has no idea of what it's talking about on many different fronts.

Oh this land of the filthy rich, where so many are homeless, and so many are jobless, and America has become an eyesore to other nations for not taking care for its own. It is an outrage that with the circumstances in this country and with the needs of the people in this country that this rich nation and its government still has the impudence to try and tell others how to run their affairs when their own house is not in order. When you don't take care of the people in your own country that depend on you, then your affairs aren't in order, and simply put you don't care. When the next missile system seems more important than it is to build a healthcare system for your citizens, then your affairs aren't in order, and that's not caring. When this government spends more on going after something that has proven wrong many times over than they do about having American families being able to provide food for their families, then America's house is not in order, and that is not a caring nation by any stretch of the imagination.

Oh how they can fabricate stories for that is something that seems to come so easily. Anything that does not deal in reality is a charm to them indeed, but to come forward with a little respect, just a little to tell the American people the truth and help them out, well that seems to be just too much for you to do, so no, your affairs are not in order, and that means your house is crumbling too. Fantasy is a thing like your arrogance that you always take too far, that you seem to be obsessed with. But just like your arrogance, when you live in a dream world you can't help but make mistakes, and even after all the mistakes that this country has made, it refuses to leave its fantasy world where mistakes are so commonly made; where the overabundance creates a lack of abundance for its elderly, its poor and its disenfranchised too. Mistakes like these are costly unless they're not mistakes, and if not mistakes, then they become more horrific, just like before. Shame on you, America, for letting your fantasy pervade.

Weapons of mass destruction: here we are over five years later and no weapons of mass destructions have ever been found in that country of Iraq, the country where the United States of America did that preemptive strike. No weapons of mass destruction, the American people and people from nations all over the world demonstrated, saying no to war. Millions of voices were heard, but America refused to listen to those voices telling it not to go to war. Other countries tried to tell you to wait, to listen to what the UN had advised and was advising you, but no, America's arrogance raised its ugly head even higher and they said they didn't care, that they would go it alone – such arrogance. Arrogance causes mistakes and problems, and this time so far it is said that at least 1,562 American soldiers have died and 11,888 American soldiers have been serious injured as of April 19, 2005 on this website, http://icasualties.org/oif/. It is estimated that over 3,000 Iraq soldiers have been killed, but the number of innocent Iraqi civilians killed is somewhere between 20,000 and 22,000 as of April 20, 2005 on this web site: http://www.iraqbodycount.net/. This website calls it U.S. led military intervention, but it is still murder when innocent men, women and children are killed. This figure doesn't include those Iraqi civilians and soldiers that have been seriously wounded, nor does it give an account of mass destruction of other kinds in that country. And all this is because the president of the United States of America, backed by his republican administration, kept spreading a boldfaced lie that kept stating over and over that there were weapons of mass destruction in Iraq. Weapons of mass destruction, none found in Iraq, the president of the United States of America lied, and the blood is now on America's hands, the blood drips, but again this is nothing new, look at the American Indians, and look at the slave ships, then look at the slavery in this country – what a history. One would think that what was done to the American Indians and what was done to the Black people that were taken from Africa would be enough, but evidently America's greed and thirst for blood is such that they must keep killing and destroying. Vampirism, look at America's war history and its crimes against humanity, one would think that this country would tire of bloody hands. They seem to keep the blood fresh as a painter does his paintbrush, constantly wet, and constantly dripping.

There are weapons of mass destruction all right, and the United States of America has probably the greatest arsenal of these weapons that exists in our world today. Think about what these weapons mean, it means that they have the ability to plain and simply do great harm, to cause great destruction, massive deaths and immense heartache and pain. Unfortunately, the real killer of weapon of mass destruction is not manufactured in plants on a assembly line, no, the real weapon of mass destruction is a mind, a maniacal mind that wants control, to be the most powerful, and he's sitting in the White House of the United States of America. He is the cause of all of this destruction, all of these soldiers deaths and injuries, and all of those innocent civilians who did no harm. The weapons of mass destruction are not plural *weapons*, it is a *weapon* of mass destruction.

What an "oops" to the American people, when everything is now out in the open, and everything now says that there wasn't and there still isn't any weapons of mass destruction in Iraq.

Bush should have read the American public and the other millions of people's lips from around the world, yes, he should have read the American people's lips when they said that there were no weapons of mass destruction, just as his father told the American people many years ago, "Read my lips". Well, the American people and the world of people now say to you Mr. President Bush, "Read Our Lips," there weren't any weapons of mass destruction and there still isn't any weapons of mass destruction!

What do you say to thousands of American families who have lost loved ones forever? Forever is a long time for someone to grieve knowing that the reason for their loss was false, and that it all could have been prevented had not this country attacked Iraq, striking the Iraqi people and their land. What will now be forever embedded in the minds of the American people is the thought of how they trusted this country to take care of their sons and daughters, nieces and nephews, grandsons and granddaughters, but now multitudes are forever lost; these lives have been snatched away forever, and by what, a single, vile vehement lie. Those other soldiers who came home or will be coming home seriously injured, without arms, legs and other serious injuries and all because of America's arrogance, America's arrogance which made the government lie to you. Arrogance causes mistakes; you can never see what's coming because you have been blinded by your own thoughts and your own greed. You can't blame this on anyone else, this was what you wanted the world to believe, but they had the sense not to believe you.

It was the same in slavery, you were arrogant, you wanted your way, you wanted to steal, you wanted to murder, so that's what you did. This war is akin to that slavery, it's not anyone else's fault, so don't try to blame someone else for what you wanted. This was your greed that told the world you didn't care, that you don't care, and it is in much the same way that your forefathers told the world that they didn't care when they enslaved those innocent African people. It didn't matter at what cost to whomever, you didn't have to pay anything monetarily; it was the hard-earned tax dollars of the American people that paid. Money that paid for your lie was spent on murder and destruction instead of that same money being spent to feed somebody, to clothe somebody, or to help pay for healthcare for this nation, or to shelter some people, and give jobs back to the American people.

The American people are the losers, not you, none of your loved ones paid with their lives. It wasn't your relatives brought back in body bags because they are still here. They are still able to go to all those wonderful places to see and enjoy, perhaps some are already there, sunbathing on Palm Beach, or in Palm Springs, perhaps others are in the Swiss Alps, or on an Alaskan cruise, or the beaches of Hawaii or the Bahamas, or skiing in Colorado, Maine or Vermont, or perhaps on the French Rivera or down Mexico way, just to name a few places those that were killed will never visit.

On March 19, 2005 I heard the president say that he didn't regret going to war, and to me that is like telling the American people: "So what that this war has killed over 1,560 American soldiers, your children, and injured or maimed over 11,880 other American soldiers, so what? he said, but Iraq had a free election that year. If that isn't the biggest slap in the face to the American people, then I don't know what is, actually it is more like spitting in their faces – it's dirtier and nastier. And thinking of free elections, one has to just think back to our own 2000 election, and 2004's election to wonder how free the election in Iraq was, especially if it were anything like our past two national elections. This "so what" attitude of the Caucasoid race is got to stop, it is murdering thousands of people. It wasn't his daughters that were killed, it wasn't his daughters that were maimed, and it wasn't even this Republican administration's sons or daughters that were killed or maimed. Perhaps this administration would not have continued to display such a "so what" arrogant attitude if it involved something that was close to their hearts. But again, one must ask, what heart? A nation with a heart and a nation that cared wouldn't be so oblivious to its people.

For a leader to make such an arrogant statement is deplorable, it was as if he was telling the American people and people around the world: "So what, yes we did it, and yes we'd do it again." Making a statement like that shows that you have no regrets, so you see the danger is still lurking, and boastfully so. Perhaps the world will answer, but I don't think that this administration will like the answer that it will be given. This head of this administration, this president is pushing this world into a more dangerous situation for the world sees him as a very dangerous fellow.

My country tis of thee, but they wouldn't tell you what they did, oh no! They can be arrogant, and that they are, but they can't own up to what they did. Why not, where is their strength of arrogance, that nobility that they try to make the world believe they have? But they can't admit to their own transgressions, they can't tell the truth – why, why can't this arrogant nation tell the truth? I will tell you why; they don't want to tell the truth because they can't. Their truth is made up of the compounded lies that they continue to tell, and it is because they are weak when it comes to truth for they have no substance, this nation is like a weak impotent man that can't get it up, they're weak. When they do something, they need ammunition to make it work. They'd like everyone to believe in all that they do based on what they say, but when others find out what their truth is based on, what this lie is based on, then they shrivel up because that medicine won't continue to work, and they've been found out, so they must hide because after they've done it, they can no longer stand, but they do have balls if nothing else.

One has to believe that if America didn't tell the truth about weapons of mass destruction, then they probably didn't tell the truth about so many other things as well. It would be totally naïve and irresponsible to believe that this was the first time that the administration, that this American government, had lied about something.

One has to wonder what they covered up, why they covered it up, and what else has been covered up to keep the American people and the world in the dark, or keep them from finding out what else this country is really involved in.

The preemptive strike was in essence like: "If you drop your weapons first, then I'll drop mine." Wrong, first the weapons of mass destruction didn't exist, but the American soldiers still fired their weapons first, and then the Iraqi soldiers fired back to defend their country from unlawful attack, the same as would happen if the situation was reversed. This country and no other country would just let their land be attacked without trying to defend it.

This nation, and this administration, makes one think in a way that's like catching your breath. As the war, which was supposed to have ended some time ago, still continues with more American soldiers being killed, the thought continues to linger, why? This administration lied, we know it, and the whole world knows it now, but this war continues adding bloodshed and more body bags to a number that is already far too great. With all that you've read, with all that you continue to hear and see on the news media, one has to almost take a deep breath to try and comprehend that American troops are still in Iraq. They are still there, still being killed, still being wounded, but it was said that this war was over just about six years ago, but America is still in Iraq, this is very disturbing. It would seem that even an administration like this one, though thoughtless, would finally say: "This has got to stop." One would think that as thoughtless as they are for their concerns of the American families, that this really has gone on far too long; but they are not saying that, and that makes me wonder, that makes me very suspicious, not just how long but what else do they have up their sleeves for the American people and for the world? Things like this really make me take a deep breath. One thing that is known is that after this last request for war based on a lie, based on invalid evidence, America cannot be trusted, this is plain and simple.

When I was growing up, we were told that there was something that a liar was, for liars aren't trustworthy, and we were told in plain English that a liar was a thief. One begins to wonder that since the USA didn't tell the truth about the weapons of mass destruction, that they did in fact lie to the American people and to the entire world, and relentlessly so, that there must have been something else behind that lie. And now, if what we learned as young adults is true, that a liar is a thief, what has the USA stolen, or what are they about to steel and claim to be theirs?

You see my thoughts keep going back to the American Indian and how the USA acquired this land. It also makes me think about slavery and the thievery of slaves, so when you look at those incidents, which both involved people, people this government robbed and murdered, and having acquired stolen land, it makes one think.

Lies, oh those lies, and to this day they still won't admit the truth of exactly what they did, but we know that they lied, and we know that they stole people too. Knowing the history of this country when it comes to lying and thievery, one has to ask, since this country is still over in Iraq, what is next? Have they stolen what they intended to take, and did they get what they came for?

You have no idea what slavery did to the Black people: one, you're not Black, and two, you weren't enslaved by this country. This country didn't steal from you, they didn't rape you, not only physically but also mentally, they didn't rob you of your self-esteem, your vitality, your passion, your manhood, or your womanhood, and they didn't do the things to you that they did to us. They didn't lynch you, whip you, spit on you, pee and defecate on you, and you wonder why the Black people, the African-American People of Color, citizens of this country, look at you and wonder sometimes, how did God ever let you live? You can't see yourselves the way that we see you, and you weren't the ones who paid the ultimate price with your lives as you continued to rape and murder, misnaming us, and continuing to violate us any way that you could, and treating us like the dogs that you are, and you wonder why we have a certain look in our eyes, a dislike for you. Well, educate yourself, remember you stole our history from us too, you Fn---Bs-- & Bas, that's right that's exactly what you were to us, you used us, and when all else failed, you used us for your experiments. Black men who had syphilis were lied to and told that they were being treated for a bad blood disorder and were never treated then for the disease, an experiment that lasted forty years. Another was the way our women were being sterilized without their knowledge; they sterilized our women by performing hysterectomies without being given consent. Oh what a breed you are, so Iraq beware, for that old saying that a leopard doesn't change its spots still holds true.

It seems that when things in the system start to work in our country, this system's evil twin, the Republican Party, the party that is known to be aligned to the rich, super-rich and corporate America, and not for working class people of America, well it seems that they want to tear down that which is working so that they can fix what's not even broken. That would be okay for kids with an Erector Set, but when adults do the same thing with their government, then there is something very wrong with this kind of mentality. This country is acting as though they are mentally challenged, why would anybody in their right mind want to destroy the accomplishments of the Democratic Party of the Clinton era just for their own gratification? Or perhaps it's because they tried to impeach him from his office but didn't succeed to the degree that they wanted, even after spending well over $40,000,000.00.

http://query.nytimes.com/gst/fullpage.html?res=9906E0DF1 73AF934A35751C1A96E958260

The Republican Party destroyed something that took years to build, that was not only arrogant, it was foolish and stupid. This country has a huge problem with its ego. Sarah Vaughan once said: "If it ain't broke, don't fix it." Republicans just can't seem to ever leave well enough alone, and every time this thinking causes the United States of America to get into trouble.

Unfortunately, what the Clinton administration

accomplished, this Republican Party was bent on destroying, and now they have. No matter how steadfastly this country grips on to arrogance, it is still not a friend of the United States of America, and this is unfortunate, but this is something that this administration is refusing to acknowledge as a flaw. This administration keeps glossing over things, you know, ignoring them and making light of them, as if they don't exist. They look at certain people as the peons; those that don't really matter, and are not of much concern, and these people certainly wouldn't help in issues for their own gratification. This country seems to relish in trying to satisfy its ego, but perhaps one day that will lead to its destruction, and that destruction might just be of the United States of America as we know it.

It is very easy to sacrifice something that is not yours because the pain felt is not your pain. Therefore, no matter how this administration tries to come off as sympathizers, it looks like they are void of any real substantive feelings, for they cannot know how it feels, and for that reason this administration comes off as being void of human feelings. When you aren't giving up anything, there's no way you can feel the pain, and when you haven't lost anything, you can't imagine that hurt or the sorrow.

It was the same way when this country forced the Africans into slavery and then began abusing them. People who are so used to inflicting pain on others cannot imagine how it feels, or they wouldn't continue to inflict that pain. These people must not care, or why would they continue to inflict pain on those that they are supposed to care about? Are they getting some kind of joy out of this? Anyone who would watch their people continue to suffer as the sons, daughters, and friends continue to come home in body bags, while they continue to be seriously injured and taken to military hospitals, and while continuing to watch them bury those men and women, and continue to watch as these families grieve is not a nice person but very sinister indeed. After looking over historical events, events that this country has precipitated, it is my opinion that the arrogance that was shown over the years and continues to be shown is a primary cause for the WTC disaster, and other related disasters of 9/11.

In a sermon by the late Rev. Dr. Martin Luther King, Jr., as was mentioned earlier, King said in reference to the United States of America that: "God is telling America you're too arrogant…"
http://husseini.org/2007/01/martin-luther-king-jr-why-i-am.html
http://lib.berkeley.edu/MRC/pacificaviet/riversidetranscript.html

Unfortunately, America has refused to listen. You refused to listen to that prophet and refused to listen to others like Malcolm X. You won't even give up your arrogance, then what is this administration or this country willing to give up? When I was growing up, one of the things that I was taught was that no one was so big that they can't be brought down, no one, and that sometimes one has to be brought down to their knees, and crawl before they can ever walk again. The expression was that you have to crawl before you can walk. African-American People of Color, citizens of this country, have crawled, for this government made sure that we were on our knees, and lower, and we crawled, but now we're standing up, and we're walking, you might say that we're even running. Perhaps the same may happen to the United States of America. Wouldn't it be a very sad commentary if it took something of a catastrophic proportion to hit the USA just because this country was so adamant about holding on to their arrogant pride and non-relinquishing nature and it caused its downfall and destruction?

The Bible tells us that Pharaoh was an arrogant man too, well history tells a story, and you know who won that race, and it wasn't Moses, he was just a messenger. If one were to look at America's ways, such as the planning and the inner-destruction within the political structure of this country, and within party lines, I think that one might agree that it looks like they do want to be crippled, but this time they may remain that way. Wouldn't it be a catastrophe if because the United States of America refused to let go of their arrogance that more men and women continued to come back in body bags, more people being murdered, and even more ending up in various hospitals and VA hospitals in this country for rehabilitation, all because of a lie told by this sitting president and all because of his own arrogance?

Here this country is with a selected president in the highest office in our government, who is willing to gamble with something that is not his – yours and your loved ones lives. There are so many things in this world that really need attention, people are starving, people are diseased, people are dying, people need clothing, people need medicine, they need shelter, people need jobs, and people are poor, and that is just in this country. We saw that on *Sixty Minutes* twice on CBS in 2004 about the bread lines in this country, and then you have those other countries where the governments are poor, so their people are even worse off.

http://www.democraticunderground.com/discuss/duboard.php?a
z=view_all&address=105x138934
http://www.cbsnews.com/stories/2003/01/08/60II/main535732.s
html

People need and every day they cry out, like when someone is crying out for love, as love is a cry that people need more than the desire, so is the desperate need of their hunger, of thirst, of clothing, of shelter, and of their happiness. America's people are crying out for this help much as the same as people cry out for love. They're saying show us that you care, show us what you are willing to do for us, for we have trusted this government to take care of us. No one is listening to the American people, but billions of dollars continue to flow out of this country faster than the Mississippi River.

Where is America, could it be that it really has moved, and if so why has she forgotten to inform the people that depend on her? When your own people, the citizens of a country, are treated like stepchildren that no one really wants, then this is great cause for concern. Those sad stories tell us how some stepchildren are treated, and we know how in the fairy tale how Cinderella's stepsisters treated her. Well, right now that's the way that this government seems to be treating its people. So, America, it's is time that you made amends to your people, time that you started taking care of business here at home instead of taking trips overseas and destroying countries only to rebuild them again. It is a cry that your people have been crying out to you for years, so before you pack up and take another trip, please feed your people, please give them shelter, give them jobs, give them an education, give them medicine and healthcare, give us perfection, for we are worth it and deserve even more. The time has come and gone, and we are still in need, still in need. Or is your plan to really move and not tell any of us where it is that you're going?

The help that this country gives to other countries is contingent on what America can get in return, i.e. riches like in Iraq, and then they will spend billions destroying so that they can build it back up within the American infrastructure. Everything that glitters is not gold, and now many European countries are looking at the United States of America again, and they are beginning to see a light that they've never seen before. Why would you spend billions of dollars to destroy something, and then many more billions to rebuild that country that you just destroyed?

American people get frustrated, this is known, but to the AAPC, this is really nothing new. At this stage, it seems as if this country is playing a game with the American people, so what do people do when they want answers and this country is not answering them in a positive way but are busy trying to answer another country? What do you really expect from your government after what it has shown you, and what do you do? The AAPC are used to being disappointed with this government because they have always come up short when it comes to the Black family, so again, nothing new here either. Is it outrageous, yes, but it is even more of an outrage to see how this country will go to war and spend billions of dollars but will refuse to take care of its people. It's even more of a crime to watch the American people when elections come and people refuse to utilize their vote, but they will then complain when the wrong party takes control of their city, state and their country. No matter what has happened, and no matter what the outcome may be, every citizen of this country needs to vote. Plain and simple, there can be no "should have, could have, would have," and "can't" just cannot be allowed to exist when it comes to you going to the polls and exercising your right to vote.

What is happening in this country is literally a crying shame, for we are the richest country in the world, and it would seem that helping to alleviate those problems aforementioned would be a far better solution, but as a co-worker told me many years ago when speaking about a work situation, simply put, "That would be too much like right." Is that true, America, would that be too much like right to set an example, to feed, to clothe, to create more jobs, create better housing, better education, better communications with all of your citizens, and healthcare for all of your citizens, would that be too much like the right, or do you think setting such a wonderful example would tarnish your reputation of being a cold calculating nation that seems to be on a path towards annihilation? But as I've learned, right does not always win out, the largest pocketbook usually does. It's not the early bird that catches the worm anymore; no, they seem to be starving, it's the one who has the fattest pocketbook. What a pity that this country refuses to do the right thing. It's like this administration's mindset is to do just the opposite, contrary to popular opinion, and continue to turn its back and a deaf ear to the American people.

What shame, if this country really wanted to, it could create change around the world that would benefit the entire human race. America, it is your call, you can regain the popularity that you once had in the world, for it was good. However, in order to do such a thing, you must regain trust, and this could be done by showing a change in your attitude, thus giving you a change of heart, and heart is something that you need to show the American people first.

The news that I have for you is very simple: arrogance is nothing to brag about, and nothing to be proud of. As I sit here on this Friday evening, in a very serious frame of mind, I'm thinking of our world and this country, and I think of how nice it would be if I didn't have to write what I'm writing, but to be able channel my thoughts and write a love story of emotions, love and laughter, but unfortunately, this must come first, even though this is hard, it's a cold job, but one that must be done – the laughter will come later.

Someone from the Republican administration was right when just after the WTC he said that this should have never happened; but it did, and unfortunately this administration hasn't learned that. It's either a refusal to learn or simply a denial that they too need to learn. Lessons are very costly, that has been proven time and time again. 09/11/2001 proved extremely costly, and the next time may be far more costly. It is high time that America listened rather than continuing with its arrogance, this country needs to be willing to learn and admit that it is possible that even they do not have all of the answers. This country also needs to stop turning its back to its people, and on those poor countries that need them, like some of the Africa countries and Haiti, these are countries where Black people live, and they also need America's help. If this nation is to survive, there must be a healing process that must start, and there must be a follow through to let its people and the world know that they are sincere.

All of a sudden fear struck this country like never before; this country was attacked, and at the beginning of the 21st century. Whites, Blacks, many different ethnic races were killed, but for the first time Whites got really scared, except Bush, who continued to read. For the very first time, and in a really big way, Whites became fearful – the terrorist had struck this country. Terrorists had struck again, and this administration thought from the very beginning that they were from abroad. And that brings me to the thought of why would they think that it was from abroad if they didn't have an advanced warning of such? Looking back at the bombing of the Federal Building in Oklahoma City, Oklahoma in 1995, then too this nation suspected that this too was from abroad, but that turned out to be Terry Nichols and Timothy McVeigh, two White Americans. So why would this administration, which seems so quick to blame, think that it came from abroad? And why did they think that it was Osama Bin Laden and al-Qaeda if they didn't know something, or had they been warned in advance?

For all of you who fear, this was your first dose of real fear, rather this was the White man's first dose of real fear in this country. But you see that Black people, the African-American People of Color, have been terrorized by the White people almost incessantly in this country by different organizations for hundreds of years, but that didn't stop you from continuing to let us be terrorized, no, you didn't send the armies out, not until we'd been kicked, beaten, bitten, burned, only after that did you really seem to get concerned enough to send out the troops because of world pressure. You must have gotten your rocks off, and also because you would have only captured your own kind, your own brothers, sisters, fathers, mothers, ministers, firemen, town councilmen who have been terrorizing Black people for years, that's why. You knew who it was that continued to terrorize us, but you let it happen; and it is obvious that you didn't want to stop it, we were still weak, and in our churches. But this time you knew that you couldn't sit back, you had to do something, this terrorism was affecting you. Your people were being killed too, you weren't used to being on your knees, you weren't used to suffering, moaning, crying and bleeding, but now you were. You weren't used to being blown away, and in your own backyard, that was the straw that broke the camel's back. This time the fire was in your front yard and your backyard, mayhem had come to your pearly White society, and you didn't like that one bit. Like Malcolm said, "The chickens had come home to roost..." Now Blacks weren't the only ones being destroyed, someone was terrorizing you this time, this time you were included, your pristine society called the United States of America, AKA, America the liar, America the destroyer, and America the cheat, so now you became angry.

Blacks had complained to you for centuries, but your wicked and evil hatred, along with your arrogance and double standards of how you looked at us as your slaves, your concubines forbade you from really paying any attention to us, so you kept ignoring us and our complaints. Again, you didn't want to take the pleasure away from your people, for you were having too much fun watching as they terrorized us. Nobody was terrorizing you; you weren't feeling any pain, you weren't suffering, and you definitely weren't feeling any hurt or sorrow, so you went along in you daily routine as if nothing was happening because nothing was happening to you. The only thing that was happening to you was the fact that you were becoming even more immune to the treatment of my people, so you felt, well, so what if they're hurting, so what if they're being beaten, murdered and the like? That's all that we were to you, a "so what" people that you had enslaved almost four hundred years ago, even though we were now free, but free to do or say what? We didn't have any power and you knew that, so again, "so what" you thought. That was the way you treated us, we weren't even treated like stepchildren, we had become the "so what" people to you; that is except when our men and women continued to volunteer for the armed services to die for this country that they loved so much, then you greeted them with your fake smile.

You had your people, the Whites, and many Blacks too, believing that you were really making progress with discrimination and race relationships. The funny thing is you really had some people fooled, but you know that old saying don't you, the one about fooling folks? "You can fool some of the people some of the time, but you can't fool all of the people all of the time." Well, this time someone was watching you and your arrogance, which has always preceded you. Well, this time it prevented you from even knowing what was going on, you refused to pay attention, even after they warned you, because they did warn you, didn't they? I bet they warned you, sure there were many warnings, but your arrogance got in the way. Your arrogance kept telling you they would never do what they told you they would do, never, and then it happened. America got punched – America's own arrogance is destroying America. So now all of a sudden, it was not funny anymore, there wasn't any more laugher, and you too began to hurt. You see there is a common sense factor that is involved here too; we'll get to that later on, but before that, let's speak of something else called forgiveness.

For those who don't think about discrimination in terms of being active or inactive, think again. Be an observant person for once and check out the people on the corner who give out pamphlets or other advertisements, check out the way a White person approaches another White person, how they greet another White man or woman, and then wait until a Black man or woman comes in contact with that same person handing out the same literature and watch and see what happens, see how they greet them, or even if they greet them at all. Sometimes they do a turn as if they don't see this person, this is so it isn't too apparent that they do not want to greet or share whatever it is that they're handing out to others; so it would not seem as if they were are ignoring them, but we know that when that happens we're being ignored. Black people know this deal; we watch it every day.

For instance, while walking down street one day, I was confronted by a White woman who was drinking a soda or perhaps a beer. The reason that I say this is because whatever it was she was drinking was placed in a small brown paper bag that one uses when trying to conceal what they are drinking from a police officer. As we were passing, she asked me if I had a quarter so that she could use the payphone. I said no, and I kind of smiled to myself, thinking that if she were handing out something, she might be one of those White people that would ignore me by making as if she hadn't seen me, like so many White people have done when handing out some literature that they'd rather you not have. But now, since she wants a quarter, not even needs it, she thinks nothing of just asking me for it as I pass, or perhaps this is just a test.

What struck me about this woman was her nonchalant non-aggressive manner, such a very soft unconcerned way about her, for she was quite the casual woman, and she didn't look like a beggar, though today some of the beggars are dressed far better than you and I. I couldn't detect any kind of immediacy in her tone by the way she asked, and there wasn't even the slightest look of rejection when I said no. In New York one meets some rather odd people, this to me was just a strange, rather weird confrontation while walking on my way to the store.

It also happens when an African-American Person of Color is hailing a taxi, and the taxicab driver chooses a White person to pick up rather than this person of color. Well, this everyone should know about that, I think that's probably been documented in every major city where Black people and minorities live, as well as the racial profiling that continues to go on by police officers and state troupers.

The next time that you go into your favorite grocery store, and as you begin to go through the checkout line to pay for your food, check and see the differences of how Blacks and Whites are addressed. Watch and see how cordial and friendly the Whites are to other Whites, not only are the Whites addressed more cordially, but so are the Hispanics by the Hispanics. But when the Hispanics greet the African-American People of Color, they aren't as cordial to them as they are to the Whites, the Ms., Mrs., Mr. or Sir is usually left out when speaking with Black people; this too is a form of discrimination for Blacks are not treated the same.

You see discrimination is alive and well, it's kicking, kicking us, and the breeding ground is hot, and this helps tremendously to keep discrimination fueled. This country has the Hispanics pitted against the African-American People of Color, it's that same old divide and conquer, but can you imagine if the Hispanics and the African-American People of Color ever got it together and aligned, well the White man would probably have to leave this country, so they keep us divided.

4. Forgiveness

I love, I live, and I want to enjoy my life, for life is too short. I respect myself and others that have and show respect for themselves and me. When I started this journey I was fifty-three, and most people would categorize me as a Black man, which is okay to an extent; I say this because I am a person of color, but that's the way it is today. The reason I say this is because this country seems to be determined to call one what they want, it's called lack of respect and denial, it's also called lazy, and also it's their way of ignoring the beautiful shades of brown that we as a people are. Take for instance your hair color; they'll have your hair color as black when it is actually dark brown, auburn, or a different shade of brown. The same holds true with your eyes, they'll say that he or she has black or dark eyes, when in actuality your eyes might be a very dark brown, blue, brown or green, hazel or gray and this is the natural color without contact lenses, then they'll have the audacity to say, "Oh what does it matter?" Or if it's a color that they don't want to say, rather than say it, you'll hear them say, "Oh I don't remember." Whites refuse to tell it like it is, but you've been doing that throughout history. Well, it matters because this is ignoring who we are, and this is just one facet. It matters because we are people, and it is our decision of how we want to be looked at, not yours. Now, when it comes to skin color, one might as well forget about the skin color because Whites are truly in another world, they seem to be blind when it comes to skin color of people of color, one would think that they were actually blind and unable to see when it come describing the color of one's skin. Just because you want to see me a certain way, that doesn't mean that it's true.

On the other hand, White folks must be really on the slow end mentally, they can't seem to figure out the Black folks of color from the Black folks that are Mulattos. One would think that they would know, after all, they did rape and have their way with our women, but perhaps there is some shame in what they did, perhaps being in denial was their way of escaping the truth, and after a while this made them unable to distinguish the Mulattos from their own White sisters and brothers. In any case, it is a wonderful kind of justice that Mother Nature has worked on them. It's quite amazing, and they thought that they were the smart ones, now that becomes laughable.

You see that after observing you for a very long time, I just had to step in, for the inaccurate way that you chose to describe my people was an abomination that really got on my nerves, and since it is my life, I'm taking control and will remind you if you try to misguide those around you with those terribly inaccurate descriptions. You see my views are strong, some may not agree with them, but they are mine, and they came to me in an honest intelligent way. I know that the way you imagine us to be is the way that you look at us, yesterday that might have been acceptable, not today, for now we are showing you how we are, and we will refuse to be looked at any other way.

When speaking of forgiveness, we need to discuss many other things that are interrelated, so let us begin by discussing discrimination. Discrimination is a very hot topic, and to begin with discrimination hurts. It is sometimes hard to talk about, even painful. Look at this country and ask yourself and anyone who will listen why? This is something I never understood, and then they told me that the Black man, the African-American Person of Color was only considered to be 3/5 of a person, 3/5 of a human being, and I went into a rage. A rage for being thought of in such a way, and a rage because of the White man's stupidity, to me this truly meant that White people were stupid. My reason for this rage was because how could a so-called intelligent society of White people, because of their own professed ego, and not mine, possibly think that we were the inferior people? In my opinion, this kind of thinking could only in actuality come from dumb White people that could only understand one language. We have eyes, we see, we have ears, we hear, we have mouths to speak and to eat, noses to smell and to breathe through, legs with feet attached to them with which to walk and run, arms with hands attached to them to hold and with which to write, we have the capacity to listen to what is being discussed, and a brain to decipher what is right and what is wrong. We talk, we laugh, all the things they can do, we can do, and some even better, so I must ask myself, what was wrong with these people?

Yes, this mentality of theirs really got my goat, so to speak; it really enraged me on many levels. We were probably the first people in this country after the American Indians to speak more than one language, we became bilingual, we understood their language, but they did not understand ours. How could these small-minded people who only knew how to suppress people and be destructive think that it was us that were 3/5 of a person and stupid? It is quite astounding to me. How in the world could they be that stupid I asked myself. But then I realized that these same people also called themselves Christians too, and were taught from the same Bibles that I was taught from, and some of them actually taught African-American People of Color from that same Bible. Shocking though true, then I started realizing many things about these folks, these folks really had problems that they refused and still refuse to see. White folks were born into denial, that must be the reason they cannot see these things, and to coin or adopt a phrase from an earlier writer or spokesperson, "They can't see the forest for the trees." It's like an alcoholic that tells you that he or she isn't an alcoholic because they really don't think that they are, their parents may have been, so they really don't see it. It's a disease, and like that disease, until one decides to admit that they have it, they remain too high to understand, therefore they remain in denial; that is until someone or something causes them to see themselves exactly as they are, and some of these people are very intelligent too. It is the same thing here, things that they did to us, the way that they discriminated against us, was beyond their capacity of thinking, or a least that's what they'd have you believe. I say this because it is beyond my wildest imagination how mankind can treat other people who are not like them in such a cruel, ugly, savage, inhuman and dastardly way. It's like I told my mother after 9/11/2001, that I would never understand mankind, even if I live to be two hundred. I had been thinking this way for sometime before that, this was just another incident that brought this thought out into the open again.

For my people, this was not the first time we'd seen such cruelty, for we had been terrorized in this country and by the people of this country for centuries, so you see I'd been thinking that way for a very long time. This time we weren't being raped, we weren't being beaten, we weren't being peed on or tortured in all those ways that we had been before. We were being killed too, but that was all, who survived, survived and those who didn't just didn't. I realize how cold this might sound, but compared to being tortured continuously, that had to seem like a blessing. One great thing too, we were not slaves, and you weren't our masters.

Discrimination hurts, and it leaves many scars; I only speak of what I know. Being a Black man of color that was born in this country and living in this country entitles me to speak about this discrimination. It has happened and continues to happen to most people of color in this country whether born here or not, those that say no must be living in a true fantasy world of some kind, and there are those that are.

5. Medical Terrorism, Modern-Day Slavery & Discrimination

As far as I know, my discrimination started in the grammar school that I attended, continued on to high school, and followed me on to the University of Connecticut, then continued on here in New York City. When you are considered Black, a person of color, light or dark, an epileptic and a gay man, well, people in this country have a tendency to look at you in a different light, and that light doesn't always shine in your favor. One thing about being Black is that you're definitely noticed, most Blacks cannot hide that fact.

One can hide the fact that they are an epileptic, well at least until that most unfortunate moment comes when a seizure grabs you, when it makes itself known by making you feel as if you're being choked, strangled, attacked, violated, and frightening you too, as you're being shaken uncontrollably, as if you are being held by someone or some horrible creature that you've never seen, can't see, really would rather not see, but for some reason doesn't like you at all, and has for unknown reasons decided that your body is a perfect place for this disease to harbor itself, so that it will be able to raise it's ugly head seemingly at will. To make matters worse, in some cases you begin drooling from the mouth like a mad dog that you've only seen on TV, or in a movie, and your eyes start doing something strange. They seem to roll to the back of your head as if you're beginning to pass out, and maybe you will or do. When taken by surprise, and it's a terrifying surprise, this is something that one cannot keep a secret, though you may try. Most people don't know just how to take a sight like that; it's not pleasant to see, and you know I can't really say that I blame them, it is truly frightening, horrifying, and you have no idea until you see this thing happen to someone else like I did. Before I was the person going through these horrible changes, I could only describe that which I felt, but one day many years later, while in my forties, I did come across a man having a grand mal seizure, and like I said, this wasn't a pretty sight. For me it was probably easier to take, so I tried to be of comfort because I too was part of that family; you might say that I had an affinity with other epileptics, and that made me akin to what he was going through. The blame that I put is on ignorance, but unfortunately people remain ignorant to this, as with other ailments and many other diseases. Again one must be taught how to relate to these things in life, one must be taught to understand how to relate to these inevitable things that can happen in their lives; we need to be better prepared in all kinds of ways.

Being an epileptic is a kind of medical terrorism because you have to try to always be on guard; you know that a seizure can possibly take hold of you at any time in the most inopportune place, but this is the nature of a terrorist beast. As an epileptic this is terror because we know that other things can happen too, like having accidents of wetting on oneself, or even worse defecating on oneself, and what an embarrassment that would be. Sometimes there is a strange kind of warning, it's called an aura, it's a very strange kind of feeling that comes over you as if it's about to suffocate you, like an invisible cloud of sorts, and you start saying to yourself, "Oh no God, not again," at least I did when I was able to pray. Sometimes this aura will pass, but then later on without any real warning, it will come back and take you almost totally by surprise for this time the aura doesn't give you any time to prepare yourself. This is an attack and it feels as if something is playing a game see to if you can tell what will happen, such a cruel game, "Now I got you," and this is tormenting your mind in the worse kind of way. It really feels as if you are fighting with someone and when the seizure begins you are almost sure.

I remember a time when I did have a seizure at work, it wasn't the first time, but on other jobs most times I was able to make it to the men's room or hide somewhere behind a counter before anyone saw me. But this time I couldn't make it to another place, like under the table, behind a curtain, behind a counter, for here there wasn't one, only tables and chairs, or behind a chair or a door to hide or behind anything that I could, for this was mostly all open space. To you that probably sounds strange, the fact that I'd want to hide, but one feels so utterly embarrassed, ugly and ashamed, for we can sense what we must look like, and we know that we're not a pretty sight. We can feel the muscles in the face moving, the jaws and lips distorting, so it seems only common to escape from a crowd that would peer.

There was one Black woman, a co-worker of mine, who saw me, she saw me and it was as if I was being caught with my pants down or being seen masturbating in the nude. She saw me, and I couldn't hide it, this ugliness from her, oh now what would she think of me? Epileptics think this way, I know, what would the other co-workers think? Before that I thought that we were friends, we laughed and talked, helped each other out, we even talked of many things, things that had nothing to do with work. I knew things about her that I really didn't want to know, nonetheless I would listen. But now she saw me have this kind of seizure, I say that because it was a mild seizure, and it wasn't my fault, I didn't mean to have a seizure, and I really didn't mean for her to see me having one. I was thinking, "What have I done?" Although I knew that it wasn't me that had caused this display, I really hadn't done anything.

Well, after that incident she ran from me, and things really changed, this woman wouldn't speak to me anymore. She told me not to touch her things, and that truly hurt, it was tearing my heart to pieces the way she looked at me, the way she kept moving away and dodging me, and I thought she was my friend. Thank God my other co-workers were nice, they were White, but they were nice and pointed out that she was an ignorant woman who was afraid, but I thought that she was my friend; a friend wouldn't act like that. Now even though I knew what they were telling me was true deep inside, that didn't stop me from feeling the pain, and it didn't diminish the hurt.

You see one can forgive an ignorant person for their ignorance, but an ignorant society that should know better is totally different. They should know better because they are the ones that write the books, articles, etc. on human behavior, they even purport to teach us, and some even with an air of arrogance. This level is very different, and when your arrogance precedes you, and I know that you know better, this is all the more reason that I cannot forgive them. As I mentioned before, that arrogance is not a friend of mine, I find it despicable, as I still do when thinking of slavery and the way my people were treated in this country where I was born, the way we've been treated by you.

I've spent forty-two years being an epileptic, that's a long time, and I have been discriminated against more than I'd like to remember. That was just one incident of the epileptic part of me, not the gay part, and definitely not the Black part of me, for the Black part is all of me, it cannot be separated, for I was born this way, as with being gay. What about my Black people who didn't do anything wrong either, it's not our fault that we have such a wide and beautiful range of color in our Blackness; nonetheless we did you no harm.

When I first moved to New York City and was applying for work, never mind my being Black, I knew that that was one strike against me, but when I then told the truth about being an epileptic, the gig was up; really the gig never was to begin with. When I was honest, and I simply checked or circled epileptic, and when I would check back to see if I'd gotten the job, I'd find out that a funny thing had occurred, someone else always got that job, or it became no longer available, or even the person that was leaving before decided to stay. Stories kept changing, so as the stories changed I had to take the advice of a friend, and I hated doing this, but I had to begin to lie. I knew that had I not taken his advice to secure work, I would have truly starved.

This society of New Yorkers acted as if being an epileptic was something that was going to rub off on them; I guess much in the same way they had years earlier, thinking the Black man's color would do the same and rub off. Of course, not everyone is like that, there are some wonderful New Yorkers that will help you out without you even having to ask, and this too happened to me while traveling a bus one day. All of a sudden I began to convulse, and this White woman that was seated beside me comforted me, stayed with me, made sure that I was all right until the ambulance arrived, she was my Guardian Angel. But still, like I said earlier, so much remains the same, for everyone is not a Guardian Angel, so why even pretend?

You see the way that I looked at my situation of being a Black man of color was one thing, and by itself that would have been okay, but the two, Black and being an epileptic too, well that was just too much for them to deal with at once. Can you imagine if I had mentioned that I was a gay man too? Well, I think that hell would have spit up fire right then and there.

Funny thing, of course this is not really funny, but they still poke fun at people like me, the epileptic me, and in the workplace too. It's amazing what you can learn or find out by not divulging everything about yourself and just listening to your co-workers and the people around you. Oh they can make for some fascinating stories, but these stories become your private stories. Now you know something about them, and you're one up on them.

I worked at a company where I had a long-term temp assignment, and no one knew my story, my history of me being an epileptic, and I listened to those jokes. The only thing is, when you're an epileptic, it's not really funny, not at all. You see you never know what a person has and how much it hurts when they are being talked about. Funny thing, you thought these people were caring people too, for they were intelligent and friendly people, at least that's what you thought.

There are so many people who say that one should tell employers that they are epileptics, that there are laws, that they can't discriminate against you. I want to you to dwell on that for a moment. When someone wants to get rid of you from a job, there are other ways to do it. I knew that I had rights; at least I thought I did, but I also knew that it would be extremely hard to prove. When you know that the likelihood of proving something is basically nil, why take a chance, and why upset yourself to the point that may possibly bring on more seizures? You must also remember that this person may even be thinking about not having a seizure more than they are about his or her rights, so the main priority is to keep calm. Even though they continue to take their medicine, they know that there is still that possibility of having a seizure, so mentally they may not be that far along to fight with anyone. Any doctor will tell you that stress can induce an illness, or make it worse, and this could make a person more susceptible to having more seizures, that I knew.

There are some really cold-hearted people out here. For instance, your job could be made absolutely miserable, you could be ignored, given more work to do, much more, and that would have been even harder, for I was just trying to fit in. My hours could have been changed, or the assignment could have ended, so there is a lot that can be done, for everyone is not as nice as you'd like to believe, and this is reality. Perhaps your so-called pals would become silent too, jeopardize their job security, pay raises, vacations, and not be able to come in late anymore, etc. etc.

Honesty has a price, and depending on what you're talking about, that price can be enormous. Then you must remember that I am what I am, a Black man, my memory forces me to remember what happened to Blacks speaking out against things in a White society. You see there is that fear factor that inhibits or prevents one from being the honest person that they would like to be, or used to be, it's called survival. Honesty these days is basically honest to an extent, but to whose extent? Well, that depends on a lot of things.

There are others that think that one should wear a medical alert, but people are too nosy, I tried that and it didn't work. I would have been an outed epileptic, and I wasn't ready to tell that truth over again. I am a Black man, and I've noticed how unkind this society that I live in can be. A Black man of color, and an epileptic, I don't think so.

You might ask, why am I telling this story now? Now I am over fifty years old, I'm writing and it's my contention that once you reach this wonderful age, for it is just that, a wonderful age and time in one's life, it should be a most exciting time too. The feeling that you can pretty much say what you damn well please comes to mind, you've earned the right, and after a while you just don't care about the repercussions anymore. Having earned this right, today I take this privilege to talk about it. I am alive, and now I don't mind being a living testament. There are many things that I will discuss now, and why, because by fifty it is my belief that one has acquired many more experiences just by living that enable him or her to discuss certain things; it's called "all of life's experiences and what a course this has been".

Being gay is a whole different issue – it's another story. To start with, you are born the way that God created you, a wonderful human being who is just as wonderful and magnificent as any so-called straight person. There is a problem because folks just can't stand the truth when it shines. The so-called Christian folks say that God doesn't make mistakes, well why can't they believe what they say and preach – that is if they really do believe it? Or is it like this, do they believe God only when He gives and shows them things to their liking, is that the way it is, is that the way Christians are or how Christianity works? Are Christians the kind of people that put God's work up to a standard, and if it doesn't measure up to their standard, then they become annoyed and begin to judge? Now don't tell me that now they're judging God Almighty's work, their creator, can that be? Is it like this: "Oh God, I know that you don't make mistakes, but I really must say that I'm not too thrilled with the way you created certain men and women. Some are a little funny, you know they act differently, they're not like you and me, you know what I mean, now that's no reflection on You, that's not what I'm saying, but it's just seems that something is wrong...are you sure that you didn't...are you sure that you didn't make a mistake, all right I said it, and if you did, well that's all right, it's okay, we'll just correct it like we do everything else, and then the world won't have to know that you made a slip, not a mistake, just a tiny slip mind you. Don't you worry, we'll come up with something to tell the folks, you know how good we are when it comes to that, I mean when it comes to fabricating, and creating stories; we know that we are the best, so just you leave it to us, you know that you can trust us. Why our reputation precedes us, why look at Germany with Hitler, Rome with Mussolini, and look at Japan with Emperor Hirohito and Tojo...just look what we accomplished, well almost at any rate. Look back at Egypt, had it not been for Moses, well...we'd...well, and Rome, look at that city, our gladiators and our architecture, our monuments supreme, we became the biggest, that is until we fell. But just the same, you know you can trust us. But enough about that for now."

But then God would probably tell them in much anger: "Oh I know what you did all right, what your goal is, you just want to exterminate those people too, so stop, don't forget what you did in this country, you do remember your slavery issue, don't you? Oh you don't want to talk about it, but there are many reminders and those that will never forget, but you won't even admit all that you did. Oh I know what you did, and that the problem with people like you is that you always want to interfere, so no thank you indeed. I don't make mistakes, what I created was created for people to see. There are certain people that bring joy and others that bring hate, but to think that I would let you interfere with more joy of this world, more compassion of men. No, first you must do that which is right for the world, so don't talk about what it is that you do, I know what you've done for you've done it too often and too many have already died."

So let's get back to this country that I was born in, the United States of America, the land of amnesia and fabrication.

Childhood for me started in Greenville, South Carolina, where I was born. My parents moved to Connecticut with the hope of having a better life, and also in the hope that they would be able to provide a better life with more opportunities for my brother and me. They wanted a place that they felt just had to be better than where they had been raised. Both of them were born and raised in South Carolina, so they had stories that they could tell, but like many other African-American People of Color, they probably never will, they will probably take them with them to their graves. My brother and I would be raised in Bridgeport, Connecticut, an old New England industrial town.

Being raised there was like being raised in a steel factory they had in that city, for it was a strict Christian family background that we came from, the Baptist on my mother's side, and Methodist on my father's side, and we would be taught right from wrong, and forgiveness of our fellow men. It was always drummed in our heads, no matter what the other person did to you, you were taught to turn the other cheek, to treat him nicely, as they put it. They told us that we knew better, and they taught us better, so be better than that, and forgive them, be the bigger person, for that was the church teaching that had been handed down from their fathers and mothers, who were church going people too. Indeed, we were raised, and raised with the fear of God, and the fear of Dad in us, and of Mom too; for she was no slouch when it came to administering a whipping, as that was what was given to us in those days. If you couldn't remember something, the beating that you'd be given would serve as a reminder of what had been told to you. You see they told us that they were tired of talking to us, imagine that, tired of talking to your children, those were Dad's words, but Mom would agreed, mothers usually didn't go against what the fathers said back then, and we were raised, so we knew better. Though I would never condone the beatings or the punishment of a child by the constant reminder that you will get a whipping when you did the slightest thing wrong, it did have its advantages, for it kept us in line.

One might say that I kind of grew up as an angel on the edge, that is until my temper flared; then I would go off if someone dared raise their hand or voice to me, I did have a mouth and let them know it. I was taught to tell the truth and I did, but when I got reprimanded for doing so, then I had to say something, I couldn't hold back, but to call the other individual a liar, well, that wasn't allowed. In those days you were supposed to say that he or she was telling a story, honey-coat your wording, and I wasn't about to do that when I knew that they had lied, you might say that I had to have the last word.

My father once said to me, "Boy, you wouldn't have lasted when he was growing up."

And to that I said, "That's why God let you be born then, and choose to let me be born when He did." And to that he said that I was probably right.

You see there are some children when told to say something or tell the truth, they did it, and I was like that; I did what I was told. They wanted me to go by the book and I was doing just that, but now they were telling me in so many words that I was wrong, or that this was just a slight variation, well I wasn't having it. Looking back, it's very simple, if you don't want a child to do something, then don't teach a child to do something and then later on tell them you didn't quite mean that, your child will be confused and won't know which way is up or down. Parents, listen to your children. I also had a look that would penetrate you as sharp as any knife and just as quick. Parents, be grateful for the blessings, understand your child, he or she understands things that are going on with them better than you, so listen and listen well. We can learn from the children, we just don't like being taught by a child, especially your own child, in fact, some of you don't like being taught by anyone, but we all must learn if a healing is to begin. If the lesson is worth learning, never mind who the teacher is, be willing to swallow that pride and accept the blessing. This country should pay close attention, for if they took heed too, perhaps they too would learn something.

Growing up taught me many things which I have learned after all these years, and now as I think back on all on that, I think that the White man had a lot to do with this indoctrination of African-American People of Color when it comes to religion. That's one thing that they didn't stop during slavery; they knew that they needed to be forgiven, and it worked, it was not only a great distraction then but has remained so ever since.

I'm not saying that they didn't do things to our Black churches like burning and bombing them, but the government knew that they needed the Black church to stand strong in adversity in order to continue their modern-day slavery. Yes, we were taught that we should forgive, the how-to part was not really explained, you were told to find it in your heart to forgive them, and other than that the Bible says that we should, so that's what I was taught – right or wrong. Being told to find it in your heart to forgive them still echoes in my mind. My heart wasn't the problem; it was their heart, a cold heart that didn't seem to have any warmth. So although the thought of those words kept echoing, I kept wondering, why should it always be us, be me that had to find it in my heart to forgive them? Why couldn't they just stop with what they were doing, then I wouldn't have to bother about finding it in my heart to forgive these people?

You see I thought that my way of thinking was all about common sense, but unfortunately when it came to common sense being used by the African-American People of Color or fear, fear was usually the common sense factor that prevailed. By this thinking the White man knew that many Blacks would in turn hand this same teaching down to their children, and their children's children. He needed to continue this distraction to keep my people weak, and keep us from fighting back. This was the plan, and it didn't have anything to do with what God's plan was. All the White folks had my parents believing that God wrote the Bible, another fabrication. God didn't have a typewriter, man wrote the Bible, and contrary to the Bible's description of Jesus, the White man had you convinced that Jesus was a White man, and definitely not a Black man; they had so many of us duped, even after you read the description of Jesus in the Bible. I believe that it was the fear that kept us duped, for so many Blacks would never say publicly that Jesus was a Black man back then.

We were a churchgoing family, and when you reached a certain age, not only did you go to Sunday school, but now you had to attend the adult service as well – you also became a participant of that church. You see this country had the Black families becoming, rather remaining, a slave to the church, this was a way that they could keep tabs on where the majority of Black people were on Sundays and how long these services lasted. If you don't think that this government didn't know how long the CME, AME, Baptist, Sanctified services were, well think again. If you think that it wasn't necessary to know where we were and for how long, you're sadly mistaken. They knew if we continued to believe what they had taught us, that Sundays was God's day, then they would not have to worry about us doing much of anything else on this morning or afternoon. They wanted to make sure that we kept ourselves enslaved to the teachings that they'd taught us, and they succeeded.

In my church, my Sunday school class must have lasted a good hour, and then if I'm not mistaken there was a little time before the services, so they knew we weren't going anywhere. When our Sunday adult service began, that would start supposedly at eleven a.m., that's if it wasn't running late due to CPT. For those of you that have never heard this before, this meant "Colored Peoples' Time", or in other words what is fashionably late, and that too they knew would last until around one p.m. or two p.m. or longer. They also knew that it all depended on how holy or carried away the reverend became, and whether there were any guests speakers and the like, and of course we can't leave out when people joined the church.

In my church, when someone new joined the church, as in most of the Black churches, time had to be added. This was a ritual because this was what we called fellowship, a celebration, and for those of you that have never heard of this, it was a time when the newest members of the church would stand upfront, and the others in the church would walk up and shake hands with this new member or members, welcoming them to the church. Then of course when someone was being baptized, that added even more time to an already long service. So you see they knew where we were, and they knew that as long as we believed in what the Bible had taught us and remembered what they had done to our people, we would not be carrying on any kind of revolution in this country on this day. They knew that we did not want to create any waves, so they had us enslaved by the teaching of the Bible, you might say that they were allowing us to incarcerate ourselves. I am telling you that some of those sisters and brothers know the Bible backwards and forwards, and they can quote it, you talk about a brilliance, but we weren't going any place, for so many still had a slave-like mentality that they hadn't broken out of. We called it being a slave for Jesus, they called it modern-day White slavery – they just didn't let us know that.

There is no reason that a child needed to be in church every Sunday for three to four and sometimes even five hours, nor was there any reason that an adult needed to be there that long either. When I say three to four hours, that was nothing, especially on Sundays when we had communion, and some of the women in the church got happy with the Holy Ghost. This was on the first Sunday in our church, or on special Sundays like Easter, Palm Sunday, Christmas, Mother's Day, Father's Day, Children's Day, Women's day, Men's day, Choir day, Usher's day or when there were just special programs, then you might be in church all day, that's if you didn't choose to go home and eat rather than have dinner at the church. So you see, they had us covered on every Sunday of the month, they knew where we'd be, and they were absolutely correct.

I guess that was one of the reasons why I couldn't wait to be all grown up, to be on my own, to discover and to learn things for myself. And when that day finally came, I was ecstatic. And home, well home for me was any place that I went, like my aunt had told my parents many years before, you "You won't have to worry about him because anywhere he hangs his hat, he's home." I also remember that Momma said there'd be days like this, she just didn't tell me they'd be so many or so bad. But to a child growing up in this type of regiment, you just wanted to let go and fly because in a sense to you this felt like a kind of torture.

When you attended public school, it didn't matter how much your teachers, who were predominantly White, liked you, or if they liked you at all, nor if the government of this country where you were born liked you. At least that's what you were told, but for a child like me, who was sensitive, I did want to fit in, even though I knew what they were saying was probably true. I was told that my job was to obey and learn all that you could. Such a cold statement, at least that's what it seemed like to me, my job, as if I wasn't suppose to enjoy, my job just seemed to be such a crude and harsh way of putting it. Part of your learning came from going to church, a place that you had to go, just the same as your school was, and you went there for one thing only, again that was to learn, that's all that mattered to my parents, and most of the other African-American People of Color's parents of my day. They thought that they knew the deal, but this time they didn't. They were schooled in the south with Black teachers, so this was not only new, but a whole new ballgame to them as they would soon find out, and parents too had to learn the hard way, for some of the things that I would be confronted with were truly new to them.

I realize now that they probably did want to speak up, but after the long indoctrination of growing up in the south, where Blacks were bullied, beaten and lynched, where their women were raped for no reason, instilled so much fear in them that they dared not speak their mind. Therefore, they chose to keep silent, and continued to pray that the day of change would hurry itself along. You see, all this had been happening in this the United States of America, your so-called caring country.

School and church was made the essence of our lives, the main focal point, and unless you were extremely ill, you went to church every Sunday and to school from Monday through Friday. You might say that we were conditioned, brainwashed, whatever word you want to use, that's the way it was, that was the law in so many Black families at that time. In going to school five days a week, you'd think that church was a thing left for Sundays, but think again, for we had to attend a catechism class once a week when you reached a certain grade level. This class was a kind of church teaching that you attended, and it was affiliated with the school system in the community that I grew up in. If you were of Catholic denomination, you attended the Catholic class, and if you were of the Protestant persuasion, you attended the Protestant class. These classes were held in their respective churches, and were the last time slot on a specified day. There seemed to be no escape from these classes, unless that is you were extremely ill or at death's door.

Unlike today, the parents weren't as lax with their children, and then too the Black family made much less than the White families, so they were striving to do better, and you were forced to do the same. This government governed our parents, and our parents governed us, but at times the severity at which they governed us felt as if they had become the slave masters to their own children.

I really didn't like it, but they didn't ask me what I liked, neither did I have any say in the matter; Bridgeport, Connecticut was the place where I was to be raised.

Unlike today, then the child had virtually no choice, and you did exactly what you were told and when. Children sense a lot of things; they know what they like, and what they don't like. When they're young, they might not be able to explain exactly, but they know. Remember one thing, whether your children can explain the whys or why nots to you, take your children's word, and believe your child. A child can see things that you can't, things that you're not even aware of; and in their learning and growing stages, they become observant and are keenly aware of things that you might not even be aware of unless they or someone else points them out to you. When they begin to ask you questions, even questions concerning politics, listen up and be ready. So, parents, take care of your children, nurture them and comfort them for they are very fragile, extremely fragile in ways that you don't really understand all the time. Take care not to interfere with their memory, for some will remember things that you do to them, what you say to them and what others do or say when they have grown into adulthood. Take it from me, I do remember when I was a child; and I do remember things that were done to me by my father like being beaten when I was little, a toddler of only three years old, so be careful with these bundles of joy.

The lessons of growing up aren't always pleasant for a Black child or other minority children, but right now I will remain focused on the Black child, that's what I was, and that's where my expertise comes in. Not being White, not being Hispanic, or Chinese, I cannot tell you how those children must have felt; I wasn't familiar with how things were in their families, therefore, I won't even try, as you should not try to explain how a Black child must feel in a White environment, school or any other – you don't know.

I have to be very firm when it comes to that because there are some White people that are always trying to tell a person of color that they know what we're going through. To tell this Black person what does and does not exist is impossible, you're not Black and you're not a person of color, so you could never see what we see, or feel what we feel. It is impossible for you to know how we feel. We feel discrimination of various kinds that you cannot see, but it's there because we can feel them. All types of discrimination aren't visible to the naked eye, so you don't understand it, and understandably so. Some of what can be seen by an outside race is often ignored; also one rarely wants to see themselves in such an unappealing light. Some of the things that we feel and sense you would say that we must be imagining that, but you're wrong. You see there is some discrimination that is not meant for you to see; other White folks hide things from even you by not being blatant, a certain eye contact, gesture or smile, and they're smart, and know that we're smart too, and they know that we will be able to pick up on these nuisances when you won't.

Another form of discrimination can be found while searching for work, which can complicate one's search, as this is not the easiest task all the time, especially for the AAPC or other people of color. Take this catering job that I had for a day, reason being, not long after I arrived and began setting up, this woman gave me a strange look and seemed to be watching me in a funny kind of way with a strange smile on her face; it was the woman who ran the catering company. After everything was set up and after this gathering was over, she told me that she wanted me to have a short-sleeved shirt, not the long sleeve shirt that I had purchased. And when I told her that she had told me to get the long-sleeved one, she replied, "Oh well, you'll be making money, you'll just have to buy another one." Such an attitude, this attitude of hers wasn't nice, it really irked me.

I then replied no, I really didn't think that I would be doing that, to which she responded, "Then you can't work for me," and I said that that would be fine.

When I walked in that day, I knew that we wouldn't get along, there was something there as she looked at me, something that was just not right, something in her personality I picked up on right away, and it wasn't a nice feeling that I got.

Things like this had happened in different ways before, so I kind of knew that she didn't care for me, and if I'm not mistaken, I was the only person of color that was working there, but who wants to be right all the time? But then much later when she showed me her arrogance and her condescending manner, it was like she was showing her real ass to me, so I simply withdrew. I don't relish seeing anyone's behind in public, and I realized that some things are just not worth it. Her personality was like that of burnt rubber, a smell that would affront anyone.

Many people of color run into many situations such as that in this country, there seems to be some White person who always wants to be in total control of a Black person, as if they want to be the master. One thing that I don't tolerate from any employer, Black or White, is yelling and screaming, for as I asked one employer over twenty-five years ago after he stopped yelling, just who he was yelling at or screaming at. When he responded that I too was included, that's when I told him that that was perhaps the way he would talk to an animal, to a dog or cat if he had one, but not to me, and if he didn't have one, then I suggest that he buy one. No one has to take that kind of verbal abuse from anyone; it doesn't matter whether you are Black, Brown, White, Chinese or Indian. If you do, then you are telling people that is how you want to be treated, you're telling them that's it all right if they yell and scream at you, and they'll continue treating you that way. If you don't want to be treated as such, it is your responsibility to make sure this is nipped in the bud. You don't have to take a "so what" attitude that is given to you by an employer or anyone, like her "so what" attitude that she gave me when telling me "so what", I'd be making money so I could buy another shirt. It seems that some people have a "so what" attitude that we all need to combat against, it's degrading. Some people really need to restructure their attitude. I've learned to give back that "so what" attitude by simply not giving in, for you see I know that I am better, I deserve better. I cannot speak for you, but if you allow people to demean you in such a way, then in essence you are telling them that it is all right to treat you that way.

It's a shame what Blacks still have to go through in the job market, and not everything is so cut and dried that you cannot always take things up with the Human Resources Department at a job, not all jobs have a Human Resources Department for the companies are private and very small.

Also there is another kind of racism that comes when two people go into a restaurant – it happened to me. When going into a restaurant with a friend, he's White and you're Black, you're served and both are waited on, and everything seems to be going quite well. The waiter brings over the wine list and once the wine is ordered he comes back to the table, opens the bottle to let it breathe and later returns and pours a little to taste, but he has given the first taste to the White person. Nothing is said, but when the check is given, the waiter, White also, automatically hands it to the White person. I remember my friend, who of course is the White person, asking me why they always assumed that he was the one with the money and that he was going to pay, and he said he'd noticed that before – and this is a foreigner who was asking me this. I remember I told him that here in New York he might be surprised at other things he might see or be confronted with when we were out together, for this was just a little something compared to other things that go on in this wonderful city.

Later on something else happened, we were at the bar having drinks before we would later be seated for dinner, at least that was our intention. We had been outside much earlier in the afternoon having a couple of beers. He liked this restaurant, and so did I. But this White bartender was so abrupt that when he saw the two of us together one could see that he'd already taken a disliking to the two of us – there was no mistake. Trying to ignore this we had two drinks, then I could see that my friend was getting a little more agitated the more that he drank, but he went downstairs to the men's room, and upon returning said, "Let's get out of here," and I agreed.

When we got outside he exploded for he could not believe what had just happened to us, and then I told him again, "I told you that things do go on, and you might find it hard to believe. That's why I warned you earlier." I told him again to take it from me because I knew; I lived here and wouldn't tell him anything that I didn't know. He was so hurt and angry and told me that if I was in his country, that would never happen, that we would never be treated that way, but then I told him that this was the old USA, and that it really didn't matter where we might be. What a state of affairs for our foreign friends to witness with a statement like this.

Another kind of discrimination that happens a lot is when you go into many of the White-owned stores. You can be shopping and browsing, just looking around trying to make up your mind if there is anything that you want from this store, and all of a sudden you have a person that is stuck almost like glue to you. They start to follow you and sometimes will continue to ask you if you need any help, but when you tell him no, for it is usually a man, that doesn't stop him from continuing to follow you. And you're asked again if you need any help, or could he possibly be of any assistance to you? This person is often a person of color that's hired to do this nasty job. You look around, you see White people and other non-Whites and none of them are being followed constantly, i.e. it's a Black issue that's been designed to keep tabs on Black customers to see if Black people are going to steal anything, and meanwhile those innocent-looking White people are probably robbing the store blind.

One of the many things that one learns in the process of growing up is that there are certain things that a person of color must learn to face rather quickly, these are cold realities that would most likely have an affect predominantly on the AAPC and/or other minorities of color. You see the role of the police officer seems to be that of a terrorist when it comes to the AAPC, for it seems that their mission is to first strike fear before helping, especially if it is a situation between the AAPC and White people. No matter what the circumstances are, it seems that these officers are more ready to take the side of the White people before the Black people, for the Whites are usually given the first chance to say what is going on before the Blacks. This in turn usually causes more friction between the parties, and even fights are started with the police officers right there. When these police officers try to break up these fights, perhaps the wrong person gets hit, i.e. a police officer, and then police brutality will start because the Blacks will be blamed whether they are the ones that accidentally hit an officer or not.

As one grew up watching and hearing these stories, I soon found out that there was plenty of police brutality in this town where I grew up, especially against the Blacks and minorities of color; this industrial town of Bridgeport had its problems with race relations. So in many ways what I saw or read in the news gave me a kind of preparedness for New York City's police officers.

The school that I attended was quite White, being that there were only six to eight AAPC in this grammar school of about six hundred pupils, and only one Black teacher. My friends were mainly White, and our neighborhood didn't leave much room for Black friends. We lived in a neighborhood that was predominantly White. A Black woman owned the house that we lived in, and some of her family lived there too, so it was just like one big extended family of African-Americans, then called "Colored People". We went to different churches, sometimes went to each other's churches for different functions for everyone came from a religious background that went way back. We ate together at different times of the year, played cards, sang together on the porch, attended picnics together, and watched out for each other, and each other's children. When addressing these extended families you addressed them by Mrs., Miss., Mr., Sir,

Aunt or Uncle, we were the children, and never called an adult by their first name, that is unless the adult had told your parents that they wished us to. This was that wonderful respect that was given in those days, and the adults could step in at any time to make sure that you were behaving like the young adults that you were being groomed to be, it didn't matter whether they were related to your extended family or not. We were the only Black families living on that street, and this was our predicament, and it didn't bother me; I got along with everyone, that is except one particularly prejudiced family that we were told to stay away from, everyone on the street knew that they were prejudice especially the old grandfather.

Some things did bother me; and the school that I attended was that thorn of annoyance. Some of my teachers were definitely racist, some more so than others, as was the principal of that school. The day of recollection seemed to come when one day my teacher asked my class, the first grade, "Does anyone know whose birthday we're going to be celebrating?" I raised my hand, and she told me to tell the class, and I did. She wasn't pleased with the answer that I gave her. I told her that I was going to be celebrating my grandmother's birthday, and indeed I was; I loved my grandmother and she was born on February 22, and this was the birthday celebration of my choice. For those of you who don't know whose birthday that is, that day is George Washington's birthday, one of the founding fathers of this country, and the first elected president of these United States of America, in this so-called democracy. You're probably wondering, didn't I know that, and my response to you is of course I did.

Let me preface my answer by saying, thank God everything that I learned was not in school. Other Blacks, people of color, friends of the family, told us about this founding father, and not only was he the first president of these United States, but that he also owned slaves and was believed to have sold some of these slaves for rum. This so-called, highly respected White man had sold slaves for rum, needless to say that didn't please me or make me happy. My teacher probably had no idea why I answered the way that I did, but that wasn't my concern; I was the child and a pupil in her class. At my age and in the first grade I knew that much, plus there was something that was in her voice, something that I didn't like or trust. Children do sense and pick up things from adults.

Looking back, I felt that she should have never asked that question with a person of color in her class. It was the way that she said "go on", and it seemed as if that tone she used was telling me, "Go ahead, see if you can answer, I know you don't know the answer, but to show you that I'm fair, I'll call on you." But then of course she wasn't expecting the answer that came from my lips. She wasn't in control; this time I was the one that duped her.

You see Black students were always being tested, and at times some teachers did say, "I'm going to be fair and call on you, and let you try and answer the question." Well, what does that statement tell you about a teacher that says that he or she's going to be fair and let a student, a minority student mind you, try and answer a question? Well, simply put, that tells me that evidently he or she wasn't being fair all the time, or one would not have any need to clarify their statement to a minority student in the class with a statement as such. The White students were never tested as such, so they weren't subject to this kind of mental abuse, plain and simple this was mental terrorism because there was something in her voice, something that was different when engaging with a Black child, and it always brought up my defenses. We had to be on guard for we knew the game that was being played, so you had to either back down for fear of being wrong, or you had to outsmart your own teacher, and in many cases that wasn't hard to do. Some students that were afraid to accept this challenge decided that it would be better not to be embarrassed should they be wrong, and that's how this mental terrorism succeeded in these innocent children; it was destroying the confidence that they had, now fear was taking its place. Those that are arrogant and think themselves to be superior miss out on things that are of importance.

Being a very sensitive young man, though a child, I felt that my sensitivity as a Black child should have been taken into consideration, this was something that she should have familiarized herself with, but evidently we were both young then, or were we? It was unfortunate that Black history wasn't a part of the Bridgeport, Connecticut school curriculum – this I would only find that out later.

First off, when a man owning slaves takes some of those slaves and sells them for some rum, this is a shameful act all by itself. And then when one thinks that people should have respect for such a scoundrel, a man on the level of a dog in my opinion, then there is something very wrong with that way of thinking. I guess I did know something about that way back then, even though I was just a child, for I knew that I would not be celebrating his birthday then or now. White folks really don't get it, and yet they keep telling themselves that they are more intelligent that Black people, now that's quite laughable.

The grading system that was used was basically geared for White students in the north, for it favored them rather than us, and while we faced a double standard in that system, our Black sisters and brothers who were students in the south were facing a different sort of abuse. Theirs was brutal physical abuse with the Civil Rights marches and demonstrations, so growing up in the north did have its advantages, that's if one would call trading for a different kind of terrorism an advantage. Looking at the differences now, what I see is hatred that was on the outside of schools in the south, and hatred that was on the inside of the schools in the north. It was a place where children were sent so that they could learn, but the effect that this had on some students was much more devastating; those students were being affected mentally, for it effected the way they learned by the way they were not being taught. It really makes one wonder how some of those students made it through it all. Well, unfortunately, some didn't make it through. While we were in an integrated school system, we lost a great part of our history, as Black history wasn't taught in the northern schools, at least not in the Bridgeport, Connecticut school system, but it was still being taught in the southern schools because many of the schools and teachers were predominately Black and they taught it. In the north we were robbed of that part of our heritage. It seems that White people just weren't concerned with what they took from Black people or denied us; it's that "so what" attitude that always seems to shine through in respect to the African-American People of Color.

Simply, this country has a way of just overlooking what they want when it pleases them. Someone told me that this is what is called amnesia, or simply put, the United States of Amnesia, and she wasn't the only one; I'd heard that expression many times before, the elderly gentleman called it a kind of historical amnesia. I never understood how a government which was so arrogant could be so proud of things that happened to the African-American People of Color and the Indians in this country, things that they caused to happen, then allowed to continue happening time and time again, and foster its growth. Being the main reason for the cause of something happening in a derogatory sense, and then refusing to take full responsibility for these things by admitting to such actions, shows again the degree of the arrogance of this government in this country called the United States of America. This is a country that pretends to play the roll an arrogant king or queen, something that has not come to fruition yet. This same government, a government presumably for the people, by the people, and of the people is supposed to be a democratic society in which everyone has a voice. Do you and do they really believe that crock of BS, do you? It makes one wonder, do they even know what their real history is, and what a disgrace they have become all over the world?

This country, the United States of America/Amnesia has a strange way of understanding. What do they want or expect other countries to admire them for, more so what do they want me to admire them for? Almost four hundred years ago, after they arrived, they have been murdering people, yes that's exactly what they've been doing ever since they began to occupy this home of the brave, and yes, it's been almost four hundred years. This country was not given to them; neither did they discover it, for as Dick Gregory said many years ago, "How do you discover something that's already occupied?"
http://www.hippy.com/php/article-114.html

Look what's happening now with Iraq, look at the similarities to what was done to the American Indians and the price that they are still paying after being robbed, and then look at what's being done in Iraq when the American touches something. Look at the horrors and listen to the Iraqi people as shown on shows like *Sixty Minutes*. Look on the Internet.

PART II

6. Looking at Forgiveness

Forgiveness is something that must be earned, but before it can be earned, atonements must be made, and before that can be accomplished, there must be an admission of things that were done, those wrongs that were grievously committed must be addressed out in the open to the American public and to the entire world and not behind closed doors. This is not something that will be allowed to continue to be glossed over and continue to be pushed further underneath an already filthy rug. To my knowledge this has never been done; this government must admit their wrongdoings and begin to repay, there must be some kind of reparation. This government of the United States of America must first admit to their wrongdoings, they must say that they are truly sorry, and there must be a repayment to the African-American People of Color that they have wronged in this country, and those that they forced here in bondage. The sins of the fathers, which are great and grave, they must be admitted to, otherwise there is no going forward, and no real healing that can begin. If one never admits to his or her wrongs, why should they be forgiven? Look at your church teaching. Why should we believe in a governmental system that continues to ignore what the African-American People of Color have gone through since being enslaved by a country so arrogant, why should we forgive them? There must be a reason to forgive; forgiveness for forgiveness sake is meaningless. I once heard a man say that whomever said forgive and forget is a damn fool, for it should have been forgive, but remember so you won't allow it to happen again.

I'm not even talking about forgetting because we all know that would be an impossibility; there are too many memories to allow one to ever forget. So if you forgive a government for something like these atrocities, these immense shameful atrocities that have been committed over hundreds of years against the African-American People of Color, then to me you have already condoned the acts that have already been committed no matter how long ago, thus giving them permission to keep on doing so, to continue treating the African-American People of Color the same way, and with no respect. To have never said that they were sorry, never to have admitted that slavery was a cruel and unusual treatment, and that it was a crime against humanity, is a crime in itself, and it remains a cruel and unusual punishment. Never to say that one is sorry, never to admit to such a terrible wrong is inexcusable, it's the intolerable height of arrogance, so to forgive, I must say unequivocally no. How in the world can one expect such when one has violated the African-American People of Color in so many ways, and not by accident? Look at the crimes for that's what they were, they were beyond criminal, but these unspeakable crimes were allowed to go unpunished, so one should never expect to be forgiven without a total admission and atonement, for without this, it remains impossible for a real healing to begin, and the AAPC remain without closure.

You teach children to tell the truth and to admit when they are wrong when they are young, I was taught this. Are you telling me that this country, this government of the United States of America, which is made up of people like you and me should not tell the truth or admit to their wrongs, that they are above the people that they have wronged, that they should not admit their wrongdoings and apologize? Is this what you are telling me, and is this going to be the continued practice, the continued double standard policy of this government? Should parents and the church stop teaching about telling the truth, and about the admission of sins? If that's what you are saying, you are in essence saying that the truth and admission of the truth doesn't matter, and it no longer needs to be divulged, if that is the case, then there would be no need of forgiveness because there wouldn't be any reason to forgive if the truth didn't have to be known. Can you imagine what that would do to the American judicial system? There would be no need to go before a judge and raise your right hand on this man-written Bible and swear to tell the whole what. What would happen, that would truly leave the American judicial system in a bind, people would be coming to court saying, "Your honor, now I don't have to tell the truth, since this government made it that way, I really don't understand why we are here. Why are you looking at me in such a strange way, why, didn't you hear what happened? You mean nobody told you that since the government of the United States of America doesn't have to admit their guilt, admit to their wrongdoings or tell the truth, that the American people have decided to stop teaching it in school, and you know since everybody knows by now, that the White man wrote the Bible, the churches also decided that it was no longer necessary to divulge the truth or forgive. That was a landmark decision, and that decision was based on the Arrogance of The United States of America vs. the African-American People of Color, Amnesia vs. Honesty, and it was based on the fact that the United States of America refuses to admit that slavery was a cruel and unusual treatment, and that it was a crime against humanity and they refuse to apologize. Your honor, you mean to say that they forgot to tell even you, oh well that must have been that old amnesia of theirs at work again."

Growing up in a country that is filled with so much hatred and jealousy of the Black man, hatred of people of color, hatred of people who are not as you are, a White race of people inclusive of the so-called straight White man as he'd like us to believe, is very hard to say the least. This is a very racist and violent country; both Whites and Blacks are racist. I can understand to some degree or perhaps to a large degree the racism on the part of the Blacks against Whites; what I don't understand is the racism on the part of the Whites that has been placed against the Blacks. The Black man didn't rape your great-great-grandmothers, sisters and brothers, and the Black man didn't beat your men, women, and children, or steal your children. The Black man didn't cut off the sex of your White men either, neither did they sterilize your women, or use your people for experiments as was done to the Black men in Tuskegee, Alabama in the 20th century. Nor did he prevent your people from learning, reading, writing, getting an education, and most certainly he didn't murder your people as you have murdered my people, from the very time that you bought or stole them from Africa, or when you thought that he looked at your women the wrong way, or perhaps answered you the wrong way, telling you where to go, no, that blood is not on our hands. You think that the country you are born in is your own country, when in fact it's a country that you stole from the people who still live here. After all that you have done, you still refuse to really own up to the blood that's on your hands, and it's still dripping, what a shameless people you are.

The grammar school that I attended was racist. It was a school that allowed one of the White teachers to call me a nigger, and there was no real reprimand for she was not really disciplined. But because of me losing my temper and calling her a White bitch, I was sent home, and one of my parents had to go to see the principal before I was allowed to return to my classroom and classes. Mind you, I was never allowed to swear growing up, that language wasn't allowed, and though my parents understood why I lost my temper, they did reprimand me for sinking to such a level of a poor White woman. I was told when a dog wallows in the mud that I didn't have to do the same, for then I was no better than they were. If you wallow in the mud with pigs, you come up smelling like the swine they are.

The high school that I attended had the same bad element, there was another White teacher that called me the same name, and once again one of my parents had to go there and speak to see one of the assistant principals before I was allowed to return to class.

This was one of the problems that plagued Black students in a racist predominately White environment in the northern schools, and this was something new to Black parents from the south who grew up in Black schools because they had never faced anything like this, this was all new to them. Mind you, these two teachers that I speak of were not only White, but they were also women, perhaps they had some kind of fixation on the Black male.

This country has a problem with its regrets, even to this day they don't want to own up to them, or perhaps they don't feel that any regrets exist, and if that is the case, then they are in a much sorrier mental state than I had imagined. But if you or I were to go before a court of law, and if we had done something unlawful, then they would expect us to be charged and expect that we plead guilty to those charges. However, here in the same country, in USA, where the White man created those laws, it seems as if they're being allowed to refuse to plead guilty as charged to their own law, there's a double standard, and that's the way it's always been when putting Blacks against Whites in school or out, at work, or in our daily lives. The laws in this country don't seem to be applicable to everyone in the same way. Equality in this country really doesn't seem to have much meaning at all, other than to say, well, it sounds good, and it looks good on paper. It also helps when they are writing lyrics for songs, and words for documentaries about this country. Oh, it is a wonderful word to hear, but just like the word "love", if you don't show it, then it doesn't mean a thing – it's just a pretty word to me.

7. But You're Different

Expressions that people use can be some of the dumbest, most ridiculous, and demeaning statements that can come from the mouths of people. But there is one particular expression that I've heard come out of the mouths of primarily White people, and that expression is: "Oh, but you're different." Now what the hell is that supposed to mean? It's really annoying when someone has the audacity to say something like that, it's a statement that makes me really angry because I know from experience that this is meant as a distinction to separate one from what they really don't particularly like at all, and it is also very demeaning. It's said to make you feel comfortable that they like being around you, like you should be grateful or something, as if you're some kind of pet, but not the rest of your people. You see this is their way of identifying the fact that they like you, but not your race of people as a whole.

When growing up and later into my adulthood, this statement, or to be more precise, this semi-statement, was heard quite often, and even today it still is. "Oh but you're different." Think about it, how would you like it if someone said that to you? That is a powerful statement, so first repeat it in your mind and just see how annoying that sounds, and then think of it in the context of a conversation when talking to an AAPC, or for that matter any other minority, and just think about how that might sound to them. Also, think of that same statement when used by some of your associates who are straight, and there is a friend that is gay in the midst of these people, and then during that conversation they quickly put a proviso, a clarification when speaking about something like, "Oh not you, you're different." So you see this is not just Black vs. White, it can be gay vs. straight, but right now we'll just focus on the Black vs. White issue.

So many times people don't think about what it is that they are saying before they say it, and that can truly get them into a whole lot of trouble. You see language is beautiful, the words are beautiful, but there is a danger in not knowing how to use certain words, or flippantly using them in the wrong manner, a manner in which when strung together is either offensive or can become offensive. By itself "oh" is just an ordinary sort of word that's not particularly interesting. "But", well, it's a little different. It's a conjunction that is used to make a stipulation of a previous part of a sentence, give explanation, and is used when making a distinction. And "you're", well, that's actually two words connected by an apostrophe. But "different", well, now that can open up a can of worms so to speak because now you have a word with some true meaning. It's very powerful and it has become a definitive qualifier used in conjunction with the previous words, of which but is the main conjunction. Think about this word as it relates to fabrics, and then think of this word as it relates to the colors of Black and White, and more specifically to White people vs. African-American People of Color, and then tell me the connotation that rings through your mind. Now think about this country and its prejudices, and the discriminations of the African-American People of Color when speaking of crime, thievery and the like, and you are speaking about those that commit those said crimes, and you happen to be speaking to your friends and your Black friend is included in this conversation, and you make what I call the oops of all statements: "Oh, but you're different, you're not like that, I didn't mean you, you know that." Well, that could destroy a friendship because it tells how you really think, for that is a real prejudicial statement.

First off, you're offending this person because it's like you are grouping everyone that is involved in crime with the AAPC of this country. Another example would be when you are selling property or perhaps a house, or just renting an apartment. Someone makes a statement with your friend in the company, and says, "I wouldn't sell to them," referring again to the AAPC, but they forget perhaps that your friend is there and they like him too, so they say, "Oh but you're different, not you. " What a proviso of a statement, and it shows that that person making the statement is a racist person that is prejudice against selling to or renting to the AAPC, but since you like this one, he's not included. Well with an asinine statement like that, you have told everyone that you are prejudice, but not only that, you have demeaned this man's entire race, but in a sense you're taking him out of that race of people because you think that he's nice, you're making a distinction, but guess what, he's still a Black man.

I hope now that before you utter such a statement you think before you speak. We all need to watch what we are saying, and the way that we can do so is by thinking before opening our mouths, for there are language barriers within our own language that get in our way when it comes to communication. There is also another reason, words are very powerful, once they have been uttered, you can't take them back, they're out there forever, and sometimes a "sorry" just won't cut it. Remember, one of the main rules for speaking should be to use common sense and think before you open your mouth, for it is the tongue that defiles people, and for those of you that read the Bible, it's in there.

What is irksome is that this so-called American society, the United States of America, seems to want respect, but yet they think that they can say and do anything to any other people of color in the entire world and demand obedience. We are not obedient people. This is something that started long before I was born, like I said, and that's been almost four hundred years. This country should have had chained dogs and trained them to be their slaves, since they're supposed to be man's best friend, perhaps they would have been obedient. This is the foundation that this country was built on, bullying people who were different, and or weaker, and that was just some of the more blatant discrimination, and it would be carried over into the schools like mine. Again, I ask you to look at Iraq and the Abu Ghraib Prison and what went on with the American soldiers and the Iraqi prisoners.

Those teachers never apologized, it's evident where they learned their arrogance, so I won't even ask where they learned it, for it came from the mother country, not the stolen one here, this mother land still belongs to the Indians, but from Great Britain, where the so-called royalty still ruled. In coming over from Great Britain, as I suggest it did, it was passed on to their children and has continued throughout history. In Great Britain, it was born in them like a bad seed, and they just couldn't leave it there. So in essence this country became just like Great Britain, a government that felt that it was their right to say and have anything they so desired, the only difference was there wasn't any king or queen.

Something is very wrong with a country that feels this way, yet I don't believe they really believe that they are wrong, it's that arrogance and amnesia that is at work. They think that they are above these laws that were created, and the laws shouldn't really apply to them, but they also believe they should be able to enforce them on others. They have a rather misinformed way of thinking about that which they created, perhaps that is the way it is in a royal society where you do have a king and queen on their thrones, but growing up America, that doesn't exist here; the rules that are made are made for everyone. You know there's something else that is going on when people think that way, that thinking is very frightening, it's destructive, yet it continues.

It would seem that the people in this country love gift giving, look at the Christmas holidays, birthdays, weddings, graduations, bar mitzvahs, christenings, anniversaries and the like. Onlookers from other countries might even think that this country goes way overboard with the gift giving, for this country loves giving gifts, right? But when one begins to look at what people are really giving in a society that's become so commercialized, and what they are buying, then I really begin to wonder, what do they really know about gift giving?

8. How Does One Destroy Gifts?

How does one find it in their heart to be able to destroy God's many gifts to the world at a whim? This is some serious stuff that I'm speaking of, and it needs to be addressed, it needs to be answered, it cannot be ignored. Why destroy and keep on destroying, thus preventing the real blessing from coming, do you know what I'm talking about? Have you ever thought about how far this nation, this world would have come had it not been for the relentless destruction of so many gifts? This country is so greedy, how this country and its government can keep on destroying and keep on with its arrogance when they see what's happening in our country today, and when we look at what's happening in the world, is beyond my scope of reality. When I was growing up in the fifties, before some of the words used now to describe people were used, before this so-called kinder, gentler nation, there used to be a word used for those who are considered mentally challenged in this country. It wasn't a nice or friendly sounding word, but rather harsh and cruel in my opinion. We used to say that those people whether talking about adults or children; we used to say that the mentally challenged were "retarded", you know... a "retard", and there wasn't anything soft about that word, neither in the way it was said or how one perceived it. Well, if anyone were ever retarded, it was this country because who in their right mind would keep destroying the gifts that God gives and keeps giving to this country? Who in their right mind would destroy the wonderful people of my race, or any race for that matter, and keep us from being able to show our light to the world, prevent us from offering many rays of hope, keep the cures from coming, keep bridges from being built, keep highways from being constructed and buildings from being built, who in their right mind would do this, I ask you?

This brings me to another question that is quite simple: do you think that America is well? Since I know that everyone cannot be mentally challenged, I'm going to let everyone answer that question for themselves. It takes a cruel, uncaring and unreal bunch of people to do and continue to allow what is being done and has been done to the Black race in this country, and to continue to forge ahead and do it to other people who are weaker in other countries too. To do things for one's own self-aggrandizement is simply cruel and pathetic.

Are you beginning to see what I mean? Perhaps this country doesn't really love the gifts or want the blessings that would come forth. Simple logic and common sense tells me that a happy and contented people who are healthy, who are not in pain from disease and mental anguish, who are not homeless, who are not hungry, who can afford to be educated, who can afford to go to the dentist, to doctors, who have jobs, who have the necessary books for their enlightenment and classrooms for their children, who are clothed, and who are truly cared for in the right fashion and loved, and who are a joyful people with plenty of laughter would be able to create, share and invent more, thus enabling

God's gifts to be given, this is the real blessing that is being held back from this America, but not only this country, the world.

When you keep a people starving, without shelter, without medical help, without laughter, without education, without the proper clothing, without the necessary tools for enlightenment, without the caring, in essence you are continuing to destroy God's blessings, for we should be blessing one another. Oh, what a crippled society we live in, and instead of breeding giving, we continue to breed destruction. Instead of finding better ways to live, better ways to give, better ways to communicate, this government is spending billions of dollars, our money, to find better, quicker, more destructive and easier ways to kill and destroy people – what a terrible sin. This is where this country's arrogance combined with their so-called amnesia comes in. It's really amazing to watch this country in action, the mightier than thou people, who continue to be the most arrogant people on God's green earth, and to continue with the mindset of an undisciplined child that continues to want everything and thinks that it should be theirs, not for the asking, but for their taking.

Look at the world situation today, first this country was planning to go to war with Iraq, but that planning turned into an invasion strategy and became a preemptive strike, what has America done? The United States of America went to war by invading Iraq, and why, because the UN wouldn't give them the sanction that they wanted. They went to war by invading Iraq after millions of people demonstrated, showing their distaste in different countries from all over the world, and in this country too they demonstrated, telling this country not to go to war – "No war!" they chanted. The world said no to the invasion, but with the help of the UK and a few other countries that pledged some support, the United States of America did in fact invade Iraq. France, Germany and Russia said no to this invasion, and they were ostracized, they knew that the USA was wrong, and the blood of this war is not on their hands, but on the already bloodied hands of the USA and of the UK.

History has already shown how the ancestors of this country came over under the guise of religious freedom, and how they began murdering innocent people, a people who already inhabited this land, and more so a people that helped them in this new land. The true American Indians, who taught them how to live and cultivate this good earth, they in turn robbed, and murdered them; they wanted something that was not theirs, and they still do. Again look at the United States of America and look at what's going on in Iraq.

This country has the audacity to speak of religion, teach it as the gospel, and the way they put religion on such a pedestal with their religious higher than mighty attitude will dupe you if you're not careful. Religion makes you think, it should at any rate. I always thought that religious folks were supposed to be God-fearing folks that obeyed God, well what happened? That is what you taught us from the same Bible that you're supposed to go by, so tell us, what happened? One might ask, what has changed, and I'd respond not much. They continue to only hear what they say, they don't listen to what they say, and that's why they are having such a problem communicating with the House and the Senate. That's also the reason why they have so much trouble communicating with other countries in the world as well. So of course you know they're not listening to what you have to say, they turn deaf ears to the others, and they haven't stopped.

It's something that makes one wonder if other Whites in this country know how difficult they made it for African-American

People of Color to get an education, to survive, do they really know? Do you understand that slavery had an effect not just on the bodies, but also on to the minds and the spirits of a once highly spirited people? Slavery was a bitch, though the chains were attached to the bodies, they also had a tremendous effect on those once vibrant minds and spirits, so in essence those wonderful minds and spirits were incarcerated too. They say that a mind is a terrible thing to waste, that's something that has been said for years now, but what about the destruction of those minds that were shattered by the inhumane way those slaves were treated? Not every one of the African-American People of Color is a survivor; some are just weaker than others, as it is with any people, so we weren't and we're still not any different. Does America really understand, and furthermore do they want to understand about this slavery, which was much more than putting people in chains? Do they realize that this kind of terror, this kind of terrorism, also chained their minds and prevented those minds from coming into fruition so that they could think, be useful to themselves and to their own families, does America understand? Does America really understand what how difficult that made it for an African-American Person of Color to really get an education, or want to for that matter? They robbed us of so much; they even stole our history. After all, terrorism is great at planting terror in one's mind, it does exactly what it is designed to do, and history has shown that it works quite well.

The war that was waged is still going on; those claims of weapons of mass destruction have never been substantiated. Yet after all the facts have been shown to the world and to the American people, American men and women are still dying under the guise that they are going to Iraq to give those people freedom when Black people still haven't achieved their freedom here. These soldiers really believe that they're going to another country for that reason. The duping and the brainwashing processes of this country are incredible. And still to this day statistics show that Blacks and American Indians are the first to die in wars that this country has been in, and now created. Service pay is being cut, and the soldiers are returning home again to find no jobs. They are closing VA hospitals, yet Congress and the Senate appropriated $87 billion dollars to fight this invasion, and this website:

http://sadparade.typepad.com/sad_parade/iraq_regress_report/

gives the cost as $166,355,745,033 spent on the Iraq war, and it continues to be tabulated. The above website no longer exists; another website which gives the amount of money spent on the Iraq war is:

http://www.ourfuture.org/makingsense/factsheet/iraq-war-costs.
http://mindprod.com/politics/iraq.html

This government continues to appropriate more money to fight in some other people's land, and still today many of us are jobless, homeless, or on the verge of being homeless, disease ridden and hungry, toothless without insurance to pay for false teeth, we can't see because we can't afford to see an ophthalmologist and get glasses or the surgery needed to correct our vision, we can't afford to pay for these high-priced medicines that we do in fact need, and the list keeps on growing because we have no affordable health insurance. However, this country would have you believe that they have your best interest at heart when some people are choosing whether to buy food or medicine because they can't afford both. And if they do get both, then that just means that instead of one being stretched, now that means that the two must really be stretched because there is no money to allow them to continue to eat and pay the high price of their medicines. I want each and every one of you to think about this, really think about this as you vote for someone to steal your vote, which as you know by now has again been done. Think about those stolen votes, and what's been stolen from you, and then before casting your next vote, instead of praying, stand up and act against those who are choking you to death.

For those of you who refuse to think that this country could do something adverse to you, think like your government thinks – if you're not part of the solution, you're part of the problem. Look at what they did in Florida to the Black and minority votes, they were simply not allowed to vote, and other votes were simply deleted. Really think about your future and your government in this country, and then think about your country's love and how it either encompasses you or leaves you out, if you think it does leave you out, then ask yourself, would you show your love to your people this way?

To start with, part of the definition of love encompasses many things, and part of that involves caring, so just ask yourself if your country is involved enough in your health and welfare as a nation. Then break it down and ask yourself if your country is involved enough in the health and welfare of it's Black, Hispanic and other minority citizens, and then answer those questions. Make sure you ask yourself whether you are being taken care of the way those foreigners that come to this country are, being given political asylum by this country and with a stipend; are you being taken care of in the same way? After you have answered those questions, then ask yourself one more question; ask yourself if America is involved enough in the health and welfare of the Iraqi people and their government. Where is your country, where is the United States of America, did it move, or is it in the process of moving, and if so, who will look after the people here, and who will care for the American people of this United States? I don't like the colors that I see today, things are so uneasy and that really disturbs me. Oh my God, when will America learn that they too must learn how to parent, that means learning how to care for its children? They are in essence the parents to all of its citizens, or is America just all about rhetoric?

Photography is a hobby of mine, and with today's technology, it is really amazing how crystal clear images have become. Researching on the Internet is fascinating, and in a search I came across something that I wasn't quite prepared for. However, after seeing it, I felt that it needed to be shared, if for nothing else than to possibly gain a better understanding of things, things that perhaps may not be so obvious to some without the pictures, but something that can only help clear up a perception. Looking at some pictures on this website reminded me of the utmost cruelty of our modern-day society, cruelty and destruction with all of its sophisticated weapons of mass destruction that can and has caused so many deaths, so many disfigurations, so much pain, sorrow and grief that I can't help but wonder what is wrong with this country, this nation and this administration of ours, this country called the United States of America. And then I wonder, how is it possible that this administration can really think they made the right decision, a decision that was based on a lie, after all the facts have poured in that made it unequivocally clear that there were no weapons of mass destruction in Iraq? I wonder why this country still persists in staying in Iraq, especially after the lie has been exposed, not once but several times, and the bloodshed continues to flow, and our own soldiers continue to be killed, and the blood continues to poor from the hands of this country.

I began to think of Egypt's pharaoh more and more, and if the Bible that was written by the same White man is accurate in any way when telling of that story, then I wonder what is it going to take for the United States of America to leave Iraq. What kind of disaster will it take before this administration finally says, "Enough, Lord, we truly made a mistake"? But then I quickly thought of the issue of slavery in this country with the AAPC, and still to this day this country hasn't said enough, and that they are truly sorry for the trouble, the anguish, and the terror that they caused the people of color. Then I think of titles, names of countries, and I think of how fitting the name the United States of America is to this country, and I can only say, well it sounds good, and it too makes for a good story, but such a sad story, such a story of terrorism if the real history of this country, the real story, be told. Their hands still drip with blood from the people they stole this land from, and even more blood drips from a people that they enslaved to toil this land when they couldn't enslave the Indians. It seems as if this country always has a plan B of some kind, so I wonder what plan B for Iraq is.

Before you read on any further, the website of interest that would really be of great enlightenment is as follows: http://mindprod.com/politics/iraq.html, and take a look at the pictures and try the best that you can to absorb what you see. The pictures are in color, they are fantastic pictures for what they are, but I must warn you, they are excruciatingly vivid, painful and gruesome. Now look carefully at the men, the women and the children, taking care to look at the faces, the expressions, their eyes, the head, the nose, the mouth, the hair, the torso, the legs, the fingers, the buttocks, and the arms of children and really try to absorb all these things that you see. Weapons of mass destruction did these things and continue doing them to the

Iraqi people. If you can make it through looking at all these pictures, imagine your loved ones, your son, your daughter, your friends and your children, if you can, imagine them in the place of those Iraqi people. Imagine how you would feel if our countries were reversed, and you had the preemptive strike, and you had weapons of mass destruction attack, mutilate and murder you. Then you should be to be able to say whether this preemptive strike based on a lie unequivocally told was worth it for your children, for your relatives, for you. Then you should be able to say, "Oh Mr. President, you told me that this was necessary, and that this was a small price, and we believed you, but after seeing what we've seen, the price is not small, and this war wasn't even necessary."

Tell the world what you think once you've finished looking at the pictures on this website, that is if you can finish it, because you will feel differently if you have any kind of spirit, heart, mind or soul.

How in the world can this country, rather how can the Bush administration, this Republican administration, continue destroying life by continuing to murder innocent people, and at the same time refuse to allocate money for stem cell research, which could inevitably prolong the lives or save the lives of human beings, how could that be?

9. Let Us Not Lose Focus on Saving Lives

There is as much controversy about embryonic stem cell research, known as ESC, as there is about adult stem cell research, known as ASC. As the American people vie against each other on this heated topic, an issue that involves many religious problems as to when life begins comes into play. This is all well and good, and the Republican Party seems to oppose this research more than the Democratic Party, and once again this is not surprising. The problem that I see can be simple or complex, but for instance take this war, it's all about killing people and those right-wing Republicans, the holier than though people, don't seem to have any problem with mutilating and the murdering innocent people over in Iraq right now, Afghanistan before, and all of the confrontations in which they have continued to murder without thinking about human life, evidently that life was secondary.

Now this is a controversial research that they are fighting against, they're throwing up their so-called religious beliefs like they're the most God-fearing Christians that this world has ever seen. But we know better than that, the American people know better, and surely the minorities and the African-American

People of Color know better than that. This country never seems to have a problem when it comes to murdering people who stand in their way of getting what they want, or destroying a country that might be in their path of their obsessions. But now they want to make like they've become so devout and religious that it is almost enough to make anyone watching these chain of events throw up. Religion has now become the issue that this country is willing to use as its shield when explaining its views against ESC, but when it comes to genocide in African, where Blacks are being murdered by the hundreds of thousands, they remain on the sidelines, and so does the money that has been pledged to those countries. They then leave religion out of it because these mass murders only have to do with the elimination of Black people, people of color, so once again religion becomes the john of this country that is used as a pimp, rather to sell its material beliefs, and then collect the rewards.

Let's not lose focus on saving lives, whether you agree with the issue of ESC or ASC or not, there are so many other medical research issues at hand that can use more money appropriated to them like AIDS, which is killing millions of people; Alzheimer's disease, which is affecting so many Americans; heart disease, your various cancers including breast, colon, brain, liver, pancreatic, which are striking down so many of our young people. Lupus disease, muscular dystrophy, Parkinson's disease, herpes, diabetes, epilepsy, and spinal cord injuries are just a few that could really use an infusion of cash to go into even a greater depth to help find cures for these diseases.

But reality must come into play here because so many people of color and Black people of the world, not a minority when looking at the total population of the world, are being killed by some of these diseases, especially AIDS. Therefore, one has to think that when genocide is taking place, there are some, especially of your religious right, that say this is God's work, and with that belief they are in no hurry to stop the spread of this disease. But if something started affecting them, you'd see an infusion of money being allocated for this disease faster than any flash of lightning that could ever strike. That's when your double standard comes into play again, and the hypocrisy of the United States of America unfolds again. But think, and really let this sink in because these are just some of the potential blessings, and that's what they would be, that's what the United States of America should be passionately working on. You see that would be sharing, and that's a how to do something that was spoken of earlier, that would be how to keep people alive, it would be how to show your love and how to show the people and the entire world that this country finally gets it, they now know how to care. In keeping people alive, it would be making people happy, healthy happy people are much more productive and would create even more blessings that could be shared with the entire world.

It is a dream, but dreams can come true, so instead of constantly bickering and using a distraction like the ESC and ASC because that's what it entails doing, allocate and work on some of these other issues that are in dire need of money and of focus, and begin saving lives, for there is far too much destruction of life, and for no reason.

Growing up in this country was strange because the real American history wasn't taught in the school system that I lived in, so much was left out in the way that history was portrayed to us in the fifties and sixties. For one thing, history wasn't of great interest to me because I was being taught that history was supposed be based on the truth, and that is the way I believed, and still believe, only that is not what was being taught. When you think that it was supposed to tell the truth and encompass the truthful facts of what really happened in this country, well, you think that this history would be inclusive of your people, but that really wasn't the way it was, and this was an enormous disappointment. It was a glorification of the White man, who made it sound like Lincoln was God's gift to the Black man for having stopped slavery, and this simply is not the case. Remember, just like the Bible, man wrote the Bible, i.e. the White man, and now he had written American history too. This is someone who murdered, cheated and enslaved my people, torturing them in the worst possible ways, and now we were supposed to trust and believe his version of history of this country, not hardly, not by the longest of shots. It would simply be naïve to even imagine that a White man who perpetrated slavery by incarcerating the African people, torturing them for well over two hundred years is now going to come clean and tell you the correct version of the little bit of history that involved slavery, that would be like asking the African-American People of Color if they thought slavery was cruel?

If that were the case, then this country should have had no problem with at least giving an apology to the African-American People of Color. You see earlier when talking about the caring of this country, well caring people don't do the things that the White man has done to us – there ain't no love there. Enslaving people had nothing to do with love, if it did, it was love of ownership on the White man's part, and his inseparable greed, but the history books back then didn't tell you about all of the White man's deeds, no that was omitted, as were many things that were done to the Black people by the White society.

So while we're on the subject, let's begin with something

called justice, one day almighty justice is going to prevail, and you know something, some White folks are going to be pissed! Let's talk about slavery, and then afterwards ask yourself a simple question, rather let's start with a question in talking about slavery. The question that you need to ask yourself is rather simple: can you imagine what it must have been like, what it must have felt like, to have been a slave and to be tortured by other so-called human beings who did not look like you or speak your language? Now really take a pause, take a long pause to really think about this because this requires thought, this isn't a light matter, but it's a rough and rather heavy matter. For the White people, you need to try and think past that and think of how proud you are of your forefathers whom some of you seem to almost worship today. Now picture them having slaves, but in this picture, imagine them shackling, beating and whipping unarmed people, beating these people with pieces of old wood that would crack and leave splinters, starving these people that could not fight back, and who had done no harm, and then picture them taking these slaves and beating them with whips and chains. See them branding them with hot irons to scar them permanently, disfiguring them and for what, for more torture and their ownership; just the same way that they did to some of their animals, animals that they stole. Picture them stripping the Black men, women and children and having their way with them while making others watch what they were doing. And all this after beating them, raping them, peeing on them, defecating on them, and making them eat the feces, raping them again, and again, and then castrating some of our Black men, tarring and feathering some of them, while hanging others and making sure that their other Black people watched this horror. Now after all these things, of which these are just a few, ask yourself why you are so arrogantly proud and boastful of these people, these sick bitches and bastards of which some are a part of your extended families because that's what they were. If you think that is just a little too hard to digest, then think about the grandchildren, great-grandchildren of those that were tortured, think about how those slaves must have felt, and now think about how the African-American People of Color, citizens of this country, must feel. Right about now you should not feel that good, you should feel sick, and you shouldn't feel proud to be a part of that at all. But is that the way you feel, or do you still feel proud of what your forefathers did to our Black forefathers, who were forced to work this land, a land that you stole, and a land that they were brought to in bondage?

When I grew up, my history book didn't say "Some American History", and it surely didn't read "Some American History, Distorted, Written By and Through The White Man's Eyes." My history books didn't tell me anything about the Black founding fathers and mothers of this country; no, they left them out purposely. I guess you might say again that it's like the Bible in many ways, it only gave your views and interpretations, the interpretation that you wanted to give, what was written was what the White man wanted written, and they thought that was all anyone needed to know about. Again, it was the "so what" attitude that came into play, so what if the Black history, the history of the African-American People of Color was left out? It just didn't matter to White America, for they had lied for so long, now it would be impossible to tell the truth, that is unless they let the African-American People of Color tell their story, and of course this country was not ready to do that. The Black race, African-American People of Color, citizens of this country, their need to know just did not matter to this White man, and you want me to believe that this is American History.

When a government leaves out a quarter, a third or half or much more of your history, when a government leaves out an entire people's struggle, which was brought on by that government in the first place, and then when that same government refuses to admit the great input that the Black race, the African-American People of Color, has had in this country, that's not history, that's more like an American fable, and it's a blatant lie. American history is not truthful, it's not honest, it isn't accurate, or maybe it's just truthful and honest to an extent, but to whose extent? But still, it's amazing how they, this White government, wanted me to buy into and believe their history as if it were the gospel. Well, perhaps it was the gospel, the gospel according to Charlie, AKA Big Brother AKA the White man of the United States of America/Amnesia, and like it was said before, very similar to the Bible, perhaps in the way it discloses the so-called facts to you. After all, like I told my mother, whom I love with all of my heart, the Bible was written by man, and a White man at that, God didn't have a typewriter.

Well, you know that he wrote the history, not according to Luke, Paul or Simon, those names you know from the Bible, but it was an interesting kind of gospel/history according to men in White sheets. There comes a time when we all must face reality, and like the younger generation is saying today, the gig's up. When life becomes real, it is real, and it becomes real when we realize that reality is here, when we realize that how they've treated us is exactly how they care about us because it is exactly as they see us. And when a government has treated the Blacks, the AACP in this nation, the way that it has, it's quite evident that their actions have already shown how much and how profusely they care for us. When life becomes real, do you know when life becomes real? If you don't, here is how it is? Take now for instance, what's happening today is an inclusion of White people too, today it is you that has been put in a category, where before it would have been just the African-Americans People of Color and other minorities, now you are included. Today you too are without jobs, you too are on welfare, you are without healthcare insurance, you are without food, and you too are without homes. You're just as homeless as the African-American People of Color; in fact you may be even more so than us, now do you get the picture? This government, your savior government, which you counted on, which is still basically ruled by White people, which you put in office, has put you with us in this boat together. You are no longer above us, your status is like that of many minorities and many of the African-American People of Color in this country, or perhaps even lower, and that's when life becomes real. Don't you just love it? And you thought this country would always hold you in the highest esteem, well it did, that is right until the money factor eased in and said sorry, but you don't make enough either.

All the years that I attended grammar school and high school, from the age of five until the age of eighteen when I graduated in 1967, in all of those formative years, I never studied any American history in that Bridgeport school system that told the real history of slavery of the African-American People of Color in this country. Nor did it tell the real treachery of America's political structure, thus telling the history of the United States of America. When a country, a society if you will, a government, won't tell you the truth about its nation, what are we the people suppose to believe? Is it reasonable that we as American citizens should believe in a government that hid and still hide facts of its own wrongdoings, as sinful and disgusting as they were and are; are we now expected to all of a sudden start believing that they are now telling us the truth? These are questions that only every individual can answer for him or herself.

While growing up we were able to watch people that emigrated from other countries coming into this country that I was born in, they were White people from other countries. As these people came into this country, and as I watched, it became evident that they were treated far better than the African-American People of Color were. In growing up you began to realize that they were able to get the better jobs, a better education, and were able to buy better homes because they were paid more than the Black people, they were White people and were not being discriminated against. We also realized that they had free speech; they were able to say things that we could never say just because they were White. For instance, if they became angry and cursed at their supervisor, many times they were never even reprimanded, but you let a Black person do the same, and they would not only be reprimanded, but they would probably have been fired on top of it. There has always been a double standard in this country, one for Whites and another for Blacks. Mind you, the higher standard was set for Blacks, making it harder for us to achieve the same mark as the Whites. This so-called American government gave other Whites from other countries far more opportunities than were given to the Black people, and we were born and raised here. This government has the audacity to say that they don't understand why we feel as we do when we speak of a double standard society, don't believe them, they do understand, it's just their way of mocking us.

It didn't matter that our fathers had died in every war that this government has been involved in, or that we were among the first to die, yet when those foreigners came to this country of the own volition, they were treated better than us. If you can't understand that, then to put it as plain as possible, you must really have a bad case of denial, or simply put, you must be really dumb. Whites from other countries can enter this country today and receive political asylum, but let Blacks from Haiti come, should I say try to enter this country to ask for political asylum, and they are turned back before they can even reach our shore. Double standards, it was the African-American People of Color that these double standards were set for, so hopefully you are getting the picture because this is not a comedy, and it's by no means an error, which I'm sure that you know.

Looking back through a much earlier time in my younger adulthood, there was a young man that I met who became a friend of mine. He had recently arrived from another country, and as we talked I found out that he had come from Poland. He was a White foreigner who asked for political asylum from this country of mine, the United States of America. Not only did he receive political asylum, but they also found him a nice place to live and found him a very nice job at a famous hotel. As a matter of fact, this was a union hotel, a very nice place to work, where he had benefits of health insurance and other benefits that African-American People of Color look for when one is seeking employment, and on top of that he received a stipend.

One day while speaking with him the conversation took on a change in tone, it was on a subject that we'd never really broached before, and it became a rather heated conversation as he began speaking about this country of mine and the Blacks who were born here. In this conversation he asked me hasn't this government ever done anything for me, but like I said the conversation took on a change in tone, a tone with perhaps a little arsenic laced in it. As I started to answer him, I then paused and just stared at him momentarily as my eyes began to well up with tears, for I was angry, but more than angry I guess I felt hurt and ashamed, for you see this was my country, after all I was born here, I was the one that was raised here, not him. I was silent as I kept staring and thinking, and finally I said no, not a thing, not a damn thing.

What had happened to him and his reason for applying to this country of mine for political asylum wasn't his fault, so he wasn't to blame. But this government of mine, I thought, had not really done anything for me, but they had done plenty against my people and me, for they had enslaved our people, so perhaps they had done something just by putting us in chains, branding us with irons, whipping us with ropes and whips. That is what they did to me, they had robbed me of my history and my passion as well, so what had this government done for me, oh, he wouldn't have understood, and to think that that was just a little of what this government had done, and as of this day, have never said that they were sorry. But this is my country, and this was the unspeakable truth about they had done to me, yet here they were giving freedom away, freedom with their political asylum to the White foreigners who came, and the tax dollars that paid were the tax dollars I paid, and he was not the only one, he was just a lover of mine.

The reason I felt so hurt was here I was, an American citizen, I am still an American citizen, not naturalized, but one that was born here, and this was not my fault either, that really hurt, it stung, and it really stinks, it was almost as if he had more of a right to be here than me. You see what makes a Black man, a Black woman cry is that this country continues to ignore us and turn the other cheek when it comes to its own people of

128

color, the ones which they have abused from jump street. And every time this government gives political asylum to an individual from foreign soil, especially a White person, this is a continual torture to Blacks, to the African-American People of Color, it's like slapping us in the face every time. It continues to happen; why, because this country knows that it can count on the Black American servicemen and women who serve this country voluntarily and valiantly without fail. It seems that no matter what this government has done and continues to do, African-American People of Color continue to support this country come hell and high water, and there's been both.

Our children have remarkable minds, for instance when a foreign child comes to the United States, he observes everything that he can, as does the American child. When the Black children see how the White children are fussed over by everyone here, questions can arise. They can ask, "Mommy, Daddy, why are the foreigners treated better than we are, no one ever fusses over us like that, Mommy, Daddy, why?" Children possess gifts of friendship automatically and are uninhibited when introductions come. They have no idea about prejudice of any kind, that is until they are taught that they shouldn't like someone by a simple gesture when one child goes up getting ready to hug the other, or shake the other's hand, then one of the parents snatches their children apart, and that's one of the cruelest things that parents can do to their child – how dreadful it is when a parent passes their hatred along to their child. That's why so many people today don't know how to love, or don't know how to care, because from an early age they are only taught how not to care, or love, but only how to hate. Both are children, yet their echoes can carry a different tone, a different sound. These echoes are never ceasing; they keep tearing at the

Black man and woman's heart every day. What they've learned was actually learned in slavery. Many Blacks, men and women, never had the opportunity to grow up without prejudice, so if they are prejudiced today, America, it's your fault, for you caused that too!

This child from another country questions his parents, a child without prejudices, a child who watches, learns and plays with other children, just an ordinary child, but who has now become the classmate of this Black child, he or she begins to observe things. What happens when this child sees the anguish of a Black child? He may not know what that child is going through, but he does notice that that Black child is treated differently compared to him, for children pick up and sense just about everything. A question that this young White child might ask is: "Daddy, Mommy, why are my Black classmates treated differently than me and other White kids?"

More than that, can you imagine how that Black child feels when he or she sees and begins feeling that difference as they grow up in that same classroom in school? And to make matters worse, this new kid wasn't even born here like he or she was. Let me tell you something, that's how my generation grew up, that's how we too felt a sense of prejudice in this country, it came from the classrooms in the schools that we attended. I knew then that we were treated more like the stepchildren in this society, perhaps I didn't quite know how to verbalize it that way, but as I watched things unfold it didn't bring a smile to my face. Though what I felt was sadness with a sense of rejection, you might say that I was one of the strong ones because I always held my head up high. No one had to know what I felt, and just like my aunt later said, always hold your head up high because no one need know what it was that you were going through, so walk proud with your head in the air, and this is something that has stuck with me all of my life.

When I was a child I could have died from the pains in my stomach had it been very serious. My excruciating pain did not put me at the front of the line, I was in the south, and at a southern emergency room in a southern White hospital, and I was just a "so what" Black child, so we had to wait for a very long time before anyone would come and check on me.

This country is all about fabrication, bluntly, the USA must be imaging that they have one of the biggest penises in the world; it seems that they screw whomever they can, or is it because they have one of the smallest penises trying to impress others by telling them stories? A nation, country, village, a woman or a man, it doesn't seem to matter who or how they screw you. Countries suffer this brutal blunt force only because this country happens to have the biggest guns, the largest arsenal of weapons, and they use them in place of penises everywhere they go. They seem to have a hard time keeping that dick of theirs in their pants. Every time this country's military is involved, there seems to be some story of the U.S. service men raping women in small villages, or some other scandal.

Oh Iraq, be very careful, be very careful indeed. Look at America, really look at America and the history that took place at the real home of the brave, and then look and see who the brave really are. Look closely and ask yourselves if this is what the Iraqi nation and the Iraqi people want? Look at America's history; look back when America was invaded by the White man from Europe with the forked tongue, and under a falsehood they came wrapped in disguises. Look way back in the early days before America became the USA; a time when this country was honored by it's native people, before that invasion, so look back.

Look at how the American Indians were treated and lied to, look at how they treated these people, who just helped them to get settled in this new land, and then look at how they began to manipulate, steal, rape and murder them, and why, because they weren't satisfied being their guests, they wanted to be the hosts without guests, they wanted to own, they wanted ownership of a country, a land that didn't belong to them, and that could be similar to what they want from you.

If the scenario is anything like America before it became the USA, be careful about your land, be watchful of your riches, your oil, for they've already shown you what they can do, so be careful and never take your eyes away from your land. They already did a preemptive strike against you and your land, your home, your future, under a guise, this time it was to save you from your own dictator Saddam Hussein and other dictators, and to give you freedom, American style. But they also told the world that you had weapons of mass destruction to give themselves the excuse to enter your land with a preemptive attack on your country and your people. Beware of what you are allowing, beware again of what you ask for, and take heed because you just might get it. You were told that America was going to show you how democracy works, that they in turn would set up your government like the USA, so you could be free, and then you could see how democracy works. Beware Iraq; everything that glitters is not gold. You must remember when America started, they acquired slaves to do their work, they bought some and stole the others, well nothing has changed, that you can believe, the treachery still stands. If you believe that the USA is doing this out of the goodness of their hearts, I ask you to ask yourself, what heart and what's free? What country spends about 200 billion dollars on a nation because they say that they care about the Iraqi people, by first destroying them, killing their innocent people, and destroying their land, and is then helping to rebuild this same country that they destroyed because they say that they want you to have freedom? Do you know of anyone in the world who is that loving but yet so evil that on one hand they want you to believe that they care for you by destroying your land, by killing your men, women and children, destroying your property, and will then begin to rebuild that which they destroyed, do you know any one in their right mind that destroys something first unless they have another plan?

Look at America's homeland; look what they did to the American Indians to get this homeland, look at what they did to the Indians to get their riches, and ask yourself what do you think they'd do to you for your vast riches? Forewarned is forearmed, look at history and study this history from a nation that claims to be your friend but who comes dressed in sheep's clothing. Look at a country that says that they want you to have freedom like in the USA, then look at all those minorities, especially the people of color, the African-American People of Color, and see how they've been treated and are being treated today. Now look and see how good they are about taking care of their own citizens, by not providing jobs so that people can afford to buy food and medicine, by not providing affordable housing, by not providing healthcare insurance, and by not providing the right books and tools for education, then ask yourself, if they do this to their people, what will they do for you, and how will they care for your people?

While growing up in the sixties, a very popular president by the name of John F. Kennedy gave an inaugural speech that stirred this country's hopes and dreams, that made this country stand up and cheer in accolades for him. And though very young for a president, he possessed quite a charming personality and was probably one of the most prolific and charismatic speakers of our time. The 1961 speech to which I'm referring included a few words that set this nation's thoughts a fire, for in this inaugural address part of what he said was: "Ask not what your country can do for you, but ask what you can do for your country." At this point he received thunderous applause, and I believe that it went on to become one of the most quoted lines of an inaugural address.

As a very young man just about to enter his teens, I too thought that this man possessed a unique charm, quite fascinating, and I did like his speech then. Now having grown much older, wiser, and having matured a great deal since then, and even though I still find that his charm was fascinating, I must now say, very wrong, Mr. President. For what seemed so appropriate then does not seem to hold the fire that it once did, at least not to me as an African-American Person of Color and citizen of this country. What and how I see things today is very different, for what I see is quite troubling, so troubling that it has caused many Black American men and women of color to rethink words and acts of the past by this government, and by you. You see that the time is past due, in fact it has been long overdue, and still the answer to the Black men and women's question has never been given, Mr. President. This government has not answered many questions.

One question might be, why is this nation so arrogant when it comes to dealing with its Black population and our needs, which are quite simple? In fact, we have the same wants and needs as our White brothers and sisters here in this country, but when it comes to judging us, why are we being judged by a two-sided sword? Why when we ask for something which should have been provided for in the constitution did this same government when writing it make sure that they would have to make amendments for those provisions further down the road? To be perfectly clear, this government knew full well that in order for this constitution to cover the Black people the way that it does for Whites, some amendments would have to be made down the line to make the Black people inclusive in the same manner that White people were included from jump street. They knew this, and in knowing this was just another way to stall, it was a ploy, a tactic, for it was designed to keep the Black people in constant turmoil with the United States of America. One example was the amendment to give us the right to vote, and then you dragged your feet on this. Well, Mr. President, though you are long gone, that was a question then too, and most importantly why does this government refuse to own up to its atrocities, and help to rewrite history for the entire world to see by giving a formal apology to the African-American People of Color born and living in this country? Why can't they admit that they were wrong, undeniably wrong, to enslave such a beautiful people who did them no harm? Why can't this country answer that? So you see, Mr. President, those words: "Ask not what your country can do for you, but ask what you can do for your country," could not have been meant for the African-American People of Color in this country.

If you were alive, I would ask you, don't you think that was an oversight on your part, for you were an extremely intelligent man to have made that slip, but that could have been an oversight even for you? But if you really did mean that your speech was for us too, the African-American People of Color, then don't you think that it would have been advisable to answer the question about the equality of the Black man? Would it have been a good idea to answer the question about full citizenship and equal rights for all men, including making sure that they were inclusive of the Black man, the African-American People of Color, and definitely to have admitted to the wrongs that this government perpetrated against the African-American People of Color here in the United States of America? Don't you think that this should have come first before your words: "Ask not what your country can do for you, but ask what you can do for your country"?

To put the cart before the horse didn't and still doesn't seem like the most appropriate action. Don't you think America should have righted this wrong, Mr. President? You see, Mr. President, when you don't or refuse to answer those questions from the African-American People of Color, citizens of this country, then that really seems quite an arrogant statement to me. By not answering the questions of the African America People of Color here in the United States of America, you are really telling us implicitly that so what, we don't matter to you. To not answer a question is to be dismissive, and you've had just about four hundred years to answer it. Why since that time you could have attended several universities and become much better acquainted with the history, the thoughts, the needs, the anxieties and the desires of the African-American People of Color, the citizens of these United States of America.

To give a speech like that without righting your wrongs and first making sure that all of your citizens are included at the bargaining table, without making sure that all of your citizens are in the process when it comes to creating all of the legislative laws and laws of this land, is inexcusable.

Where is the common sense that was used to continue to

gloss over the African-American People of Color in this country, who are also citizens of this country? Are you telling me that you do not have the common sense of my grandfather, an uneducated African-American Person of Color, a man who possessed this wonderful knowledge? Are you telling me that you don't have the common sense that so many African-American People of Color have and use daily? Common sense is a basis for survival, it's the fiber, the backbone of a people, so could it be that you are telling me that when it comes to the affairs of this great nation, that the common sense factor is being left out? So are you telling me that by not answering we cannot expect you to use something that you don't have?

So we ask the president who is in office now, when is this government going to do just that, give a formal apology to the African-American People of Color, your citizens, and make restitutions, make reparations? When is this nation going to as one would say "do right by us" and do us no harm? You see John F. Kennedy said, "Ask not what your country can do for you, but ask what you can do for your country," but I say no, Black America, don't ask what we can do for this country for we have done over and above for this country when we were forced into slavery by this nation. And even after slavery ended, we have continued to do over and above the call of duty for this country. So I say no, don't ask what we can do for this country, Black America, ask that this country finally do something for us by finally admitting that slavery was a cruel and unusual punishment, and that it was a crime against humanity, that's what America can do for Black America, for the African-American People of Color, Mr. President. Apologize to us and admit that what this country did to African-American People of Color was unequivocally wrong, and that it was a crime against humanity. And then begin to pay reparations, this is what we ask from our government that raped, murdered, abused, beat our people, stole our children, stole our history, castrated our men, experimented on us in the cruelest of fashions and sterilized our women. This is what Black American and the African-American People of Color ask that America do for us instead of us asking what we can do for this country as was suggested by the late JFK.

10. What The Lord Has For Me, Nobody Can Take Away

Isn't life wonderful? So many people think of this country, this political system, as just that wonderful because what people of color see, and what White people see are two different things, what we feel, and what White people feel are two different things, and what we sense is different that what they sense. So you see everyone can answer that question for themselves, for I can only speak for myself, I cannot speak for you, and you cannot speak for me. I only speak of things of which I know something about. Don't you hate it when someone else tries to put words in your mouth, telling you that they know what you were or are thinking? When they make a really big deal of it, then you start to boil, at least I do, that's not only an arrogant statement in my opinion, but also a very unintelligent one, but nonetheless, people do make those proclamations. I do know about some good times, but I also know about some bad times. I've learned to live, smile and to laugh as much as possible as I travel through this wonderful world that God is showing me. What a joy this spirit brings me every day.

There are many blessings right here that can enrich one's life. Hey, we made it into another year, that in itself is a blessing. My views seem to be filled with more clarity than at any time previously, that's why I've chosen this media. There is a strange gnawing feeling within that feels like an itch that cannot be scratched, but if I continue to write, I have a feeling that it will go away, or at least diminish. To release your thoughts in hope that they will be read, to share something with someone should be as enjoyable as it is stimulating. Frankly, believing that you have the foresight and imagination needed to share something has rewards abounding. And though difficult, to tell things candidly in hopes of enlightening people is always an inspirational challenge. To be able to structure the material at hand and be able to link these thoughts together so that they will be understood is one of the most complicated and demanding tasks. You want to be able to reach a wide variety of people of various ethnicities because that is what this country and world is made up of.

With all that is going on in this country and the world, I'm glad that I have a place to go. Having become truly involved with the spirit that speaks to me every day, and really enjoying the wonderment that it makes me feel, it's really wonderful to have this place to go to, especially in times like these when it's needed so much. All that I feel is neither all joy or all sadness, and I get many premonitions, all of them are not filled with joy, some have been sad, some very tragic and some just plain frightening. But with the current state of affairs, I need to have a place where I can go. Right now I'd rather discuss things that bring joy rather than continuing with sadness.

This spirit of place is something that's very familiar to me; it's the home where I feel most comfortable all the time. The spirit of place, now you may ask where is this spirit of place? It is anywhere you want it to be, and the most wonderful thing about it is that you can choose to share it with someone you'd like to share it with, or you can decide not to and go there by yourself, and you wouldn't be selfish for not sharing it. Sometimes it might involve a lesson that is being created just for you. I came to this spirit of place after realizing that God gave me a mind with which to think and create, that He gave me eyes to see, my hands to feel and fingers to touch, arms to hold, a nose to smell, a tongue to taste and ears to hear even the tiniest of breezes, and the mind, body, heart and soul with which to sense and understand. That was just the beginning of something wonderful, the beginning of the spirit of place. In order to get to the spirit of place, you must be able to sense, that's probably the most important of all of the senses, and I believe that God gave it to us, putting it within all of us so that no one could see it, neither it's joy or it's sorrow, that is unless you display it. Then there's that other feeling, it's a sensation that goes with the mind and heart, that's when you're able to decipher and listen to what the spirit is telling you.

Many times, to get in touch with this spirit you must be able to listen when you hear what seems like a voice telling you where you must go, so that He can talk to you. I believe that He sends us to places so that we can become familiar with them, not for Him to speak to us, but away from the madding crowd, so that we can really listen and pay attention without the distractions.

Right now New York City is a very noisy place to write, especially this Sunday afternoon, the sirens are blaring, one after another, and it's spring, a noisier time of year in the city, and the windows and doors that are open just seem to magnify the sound. People are also nosier too, it's like they have been let out of a jail after a long cold winter. I think I'd rather be in a European country town writing, for I did feel very peaceful in some of those towns.

Sometimes it's really hard to stay focused in a big metropolis like New York City. A friend of mine a while back compared living here in New York City to a pressure cooker, and when I heard her say that I laughed and agreed. Whether one wants to believe that or not, it's true, so really think about it. Just get out of New York City and go to a much quieter place where the atmosphere is calm, where you don't have all this buzz like here in the city and you'll see. You may go to another city, a city unlike New York, a place where you feel more relaxed than you do in New York, that city can be your spirit of place. Hey, don't get me wrong, New York City can be that spirit of place too; it doesn't have to be all about a quieter place because I love New York too. New York is alive, and it has been said that it has a fascination that other cities don't, and depending on where your mind is, the spirit of place can be almost anywhere that you want it to be. It can be in the country, it can be on a farm, it can be in church, it can be in your garden, or it can be in your kitchen, your living room, your bathroom or even a special corner that you just love to be in. Perhaps your thinking or your writing corner, or it may be at the beach, or by a body of water. But if it's in a bar where you're drinking, smoking, or anywhere you're doing drugs or something that is endangering you or your health, doing something that you know you shouldn't be doing, don't try telling yourself that this is your spirit of place because your mind is using something to enhance it. So if it's telling you that this is where your spirit of place is, don't believe it, this is a false reading, and there is too much interference where you are. If your mind was clear, it would probably tell you to go home and stop kidding yourself for you do know better, you were raised, remember? You are really not at a good sense in such place; the atmosphere helps distort what you're thinking and what you believe because in part you are in darkness and distress. The spirit of place is full of light and beauty and needs no outside stimulants and/or enhancers.

Now that I've grown a little older, I do like a quieter atmosphere, for me it's more conducive for relaxing and reading. To be specific, I found that wonderful spirit of place when I was in Europe, in Norway and Sweden. There was such a quiet joy and peacefulness there that I've never felt anywhere else. When one can feel joy, you're more apt to listen to what the spirit, what the creator has to tell you. Think about that, when you feel joy, it's much more likely that you'll be more responsive to people, to animals, plants, trees, the ocean, lakes, streams and nature in general. You may ask why I say that, well, it's because that joy is bringing you in touch with what is important in life, your beautiful surroundings, these natural surroundings that have been supplied by nature itself, and a beauty that doesn't need any enhancement from mankind.

In this fabulous state one can meditate much easier; you have less distractions. Many distractions cause annoyance, and if you're annoyed, it's much harder to concentrate. Being far from the madding crowd takes you away from these annoyances. I find that concentration is much better when I can get into my own head and hear myself think – it's easier. There's such a difference when you're away in a small town or country where there is that quietness, and when you are listening to that quiet sound, the natural sound of birds, crickets and of water flowing, or of the rain falling from the sky as it touches those different things, the ground, the leaves and your windowpanes, and the wonderful smell of that shower in springtime, such a fresh and fragrant smell. Now you can begin hear yourself think without all those sirens, wow! Now you can begin to think without the jets flying low over your head, those annoying car alarms, the screeching sound of brakes and tires skidding, people yelling and screaming, cursing, those bomb blasting radios, those car horns of impatience drivers, those helicopters flying low above for a story that they're covering, the broken glass or even gunshots. You begin to realize how much all those people and noises had been affecting you, it's quite amazing, but up until now you never realized it.

It's the same in this country, you never realized how corrupt, violent, and prejudice this country was until you talked to an African-American Person of Color who was born, raised and lives here. Now you can begin to see what your eyes wouldn't or couldn't see, what your voice couldn't tell you, what you couldn't or wouldn't let yourself sense or feel, and why, because it really didn't effect you like it did people of color. Now you're beginning to feel and to sense something that you couldn't see while in a blanket of fog, once that fog begins lifting, then you can begin to see, once you remove yourself from within an environment, you too begin to see things that you couldn't see or sense before, or perhaps just refused to see. Sometimes when we're too far away from something, it's almost like having blinders on. It's the same in an opposite way of being too close; those of us that are too close must sometimes take a step back to focus, and those of us that are too far away must step in closer in order to focus. It all depends on what picture you are willing to see, one that is blurred or one that is clear. At some point in our lives, we all need to take steps forward and take some steps backward, but in order to do these things, you must be willing to open up that mind that God gave you to use.

All that we have been asking you to do for hundreds of years was to remove yourself and your elements so that you could begin to see, and we didn't think that we were asking too much. The spirit of place has been around since before man became corrupt, he had an escape if he wanted one. We tried to teach what we have known all along, but you refused to listen to the voice of your slaves, you refused listen to the cries of the oppressed, those you judged inferior to you, who were only trying as we have all these years to show you how to live and how to receive a blessing. But who knows, maybe you didn't think that you needed a blessing, but everyone needs a blessing whether they think it is appropriate or not, and those blessings can come from the least expected source, like those slaves who you thought could do nothing for you except be your slaves. What a pity it is when one refuses to see the blessing that God has been trying to show them over and over.

Blessings are all around us, they present themselves in so many ways, for blessings are like a fresh breeze blowing gently ever so softly, and it will come up to you like the friendliest little squirrel, but you must be receptive to things that you see, things that you feel for they are out there. If you don't understand what you feel, and really want to know, ask God and then just wait for an answer, He'll show you. One should never say that they never got a blessing for we all have; we might have just missed it or not have been aware of when it arrived. When that man or woman greeted you today on the elevator where you work, or a child said hello as you were rushing by, those are blessings, but did you respond? When someone held the door open for you, but you said nothing, that was a blessing, but had they not held that same door open for you, then you would have responded. Simple things in life are blessings; they are not all of the heavy spiritual kind. Sometimes I ask my friends if I can give them a blessing, and then I hug them for that is a blessing that I want to share with them, it's the good feeling that I'm sharing with them. Blessings don't have to be that complex, they are only as complicated as we make them. Perhaps you didn't see the blessings because you never looked, and if you never looked or opened this package, well of course you won't be able to appreciate the gift.

Sometimes there are things that must be opened up; number one is our eyes, and number two is our mouth because sometimes it is just that simple. There are many different kinds of blessings, so sometimes to receive a blessing we just have to ask. You don't seem to have any problem about asking for those material things such as a raise and other things that you don't even need but want just because it costs a lot of money and your friends have it too. You don't mind asking for those things, but you see those things are not blessings, they won't make a stranger smile when you tell them what you've got, but a hello will, blessings are simple things that matter, and they can brighten up someone's day. It's all about paying attention in life for the spirit is out there just waiting for us to respond.

Now did you think about the blessings that you received today? Did you perhaps see someone that you were just thinking about, or receive a call from a friend that you hadn't heard from in a very long time? You woke today, didn't you? Were you in any pain, and were you able to get out of bed and get dressed by yourself? Were you able walk to the bathroom by yourself, wash your face, brush your teeth and fix your hair? Were you able to see the sun set, hear the birds chirping, the cats meowing, and the dogs barking? Were you able to hear the rustling in the grass made by a very soft breeze or a garter snake or hear that door begin to squeak? Were you able to smell the bacon that someone had cooked when you opened your window, or the fragrant coffee that you just brewed? Were you able to see those flowers on the terrace and watch them as they bloomed? Were you able to smile when you watched a child at play, or when you met your lover at the airport and hugged each after being apart for oh so long, or cry when you lost a loved one so dear? Were you able to chew the meat that you had on your plate, or smell the aroma of a freshly baked cake, or taste those succulent drippings of that wonderful steak? Were you able to hold that bottle, reach for a glass, taste the body of that splendid wine that your friend had just poured or open a door without help? Were you able to bend down to pick up that dollar that you dropped on the street or tie the laces of you shoes, and then walk up those stairs? Were you able to button the buttons of your shirt, or press a crease in the pants that you wore? Were you able to zip up the zipper in your dress, and put on your coat before walking out the door? Were you able to see the figures to add to make sure that you weren't being overcharged, or laugh at that joke that almost made you cry? Were you able to feel the tears that ran down your face, or feel the pain when someone accidentally stepped on your toe or simply hurt your feelings? Were you able to drive down to the beach and swim, and then play a few sets of tennis with a friend? Were you able to speak and say hello, or wave goodbye when departing from someone? Now, do you think that you've ever been blessed?

If you can do all of these things, then you have been enormously blessed because that means you can talk, you can walk and smile, you can laugh, and what a blessing laughter is, you can eat and smell, you can see and taste. You can also hear, and you're able to touch, to hug and to feel, and if you ever thought that you've never been blessed, and are still able to taste a good sweet potato pie, or homemade bread, and if you ever thought that you hadn't been blessed, then you must be out of you mind because to be able to do just some of those things is truly a blessing indeed, but to be able to do all of these things is a blessing of the highest magnitude because there are some people who cannot do any of these things. Oh the blessings that we miss in things we take for granted, so remember for they aren't that complex, only we make them seem that way, so next time don't insult God, or whoever you call supreme, by being a disgrace to His blessings that you receive every day.

Candles and Tears

Candles are so beautiful; it is a very simple way to shed a little light, and to share a glow of warmth. Most candles drip, melting the wax down their sides as they melt away. While they are melting some people make wonderful-looking candles that have been melted down by having them purposely drip over things, slowly making an artistic design. Wax is beautiful and can be molded into many different shapes and forms, and color can be added. When I look at a candle dripping and I am in deep thought, I say that it must be crying, and when thinking very deeply what I see is more sadness than the joy, for I think of love when the joy drips out of it. When thinking of death, as when life is sucked away from a loved ones lungs, or when someone beats the other one to death, or drowns the hopes and dreams of a people enslaved, oh death that has many forms just like those candles. Or it can be that of wars when the lights have gone out and candles must be used because there is no light, there is no electricity because man has destroyed something else once again. At the same time I say thank God for whoever invented this simple candle.

But in thinking about this wonderment that causes me so much thought, the tears of my people come back to my thoughts, and I begin to wonder how many candles it would take to make all of the cries of the African-American People of Color, those citizens of this country, silent. And then I really wonder how many candles it would take if one were used for all of the atrocities committed against my people here in this country by you in this state. And if I begin to think in detail of these things, I too become like the candle with tears running down my face. I too feel as if I'm melting because things that were done make me cringe as though I feel them today, not of yesterday, as if I am melting like this candle, for the horror begins to singe my spirit as well as the flame of this candle. And as I feel that flame singe, burning my people, I am sure that this was done to them too, whether directly on their beautiful skin and beautiful bodies or where they slept or worshipped, my body begins to distort itself just as the wax of a candle does as it drips and sometimes breaks off.

Tears of my people are tears that stain this country, this land, for they were not ordinary tears of life fulfilled or fully lived, of laughter or of joy, of birth and of death, but bloodstained tears from torture, from torment and strife that will never wipe clean. In thinking I ask myself oh God, why this inhumanity to man, why did man cause such inhumanity to us, oh God, why? Why is he still continuing to cause such inhumanity to people, oh why? Why are some men such a vile disgrace to the human race? I can't help but think, but I cannot understand, there is no comprehension for me here. So you see if you look beyond such a lovely light, such an intense glow and really begin to think, all is not joyful, but joy must be coming, it must, so I will light a candle for prosperity, I will light a candle for life, I will light a candle for the births, and I will continue to light a candle for humankind and continue to pray for the good to win over. I will light a candle for joy, for joy is like the season we wish to see, joy is like the health that we wish to have, and joy is like that love when it begins to sparkle. Oh yes, I will light many candles for that joy that is coming quickly like a quiet storm. But before I light those candles I must light those for the deaths of all who died in hope that this light will help them on their way to be remembered and thank them too, for as we know many had no burial as we do today. We need tears, not those of sadness but those that run like a clear river down a mountain into a spring, those that can be captured to water the new life that is fast growing, the budding trees, the grass and those wonderful flowers that welcome spring time, those are the tears which we need for today and tomorrow. Then I will again with the greatest pleasure light that candle of joy singing praise for the joy of life, Amen.

It's a lonely apartment sometimes; there's love in it because my good vibrations are here, but it's not what I'd call a real home of love. I consider a real home to be one where two people are living in a space together and are sharing that same space and things; it doesn't matter how small or how large the space is. On the other hand a real home in the United States must be one that makes its citizens feel wanted and welcome, its vastness and beauty cannot be a substitute for warmth. By not being in a true relationship, the one thing that I miss the most is the sharing, there is no real substitute for that because you are missing the most important link, the human connection, and a roommate is not the same, there is a kind of void that is still there, and that is probably the hardest thing to overcome. Older people know what I'm talking about, and those that have truly been a team as one or been in love as one would know what I'm talking about. They understand what happens when one of them is gone, there is that void. A certain look, whether it be a glance, a smile, a touch, a glass of wine, dinner, a cup of coffee, several cups of coffee, that's a lot, and not having it there is difficult, quite difficult at best. And if you have an animal, they too feel this void, for they may wait by the door for the other to come home, but no one comes through that door, then they finally come over to you, sharing your sorrow, which is truly part of their sorrow to. Or perhaps you must go and get this companion for they would continue to wait by that door like the old faithful companion that they are. As you set the table for two instead of one because you still haven't gotten used to the idea that your friend is not here, they will not be coming home to you, well, that's another trying time.

Joy, Praise and Love

Praise to you for the journey that continues and for the journeys that await.
Thanks for the Blessing! When in times of sorrow one does not usually think of joy,

*for that just seems so far too removed.   In thinking about the
slavery
that was done to you for it just didn't happen for those were
cruel acts.
Cruel things just don't happen as one might want us to believe
for something of evil takes planning indeed.   It takes a mind to
be cruel
just as it takes a mind to love, there is a how to hate, but many
more of how to love,
just as there are so many ways to love, there are too many ways
to hate,
and that's where cruelty comes from; it comes out of hate,
for hate is not natural as the love that we make.
For as there is that wonderful love that is supreme,
there is also that hate which is so cruel and dark.
Love is for those wonderful things for the joy that it brings
from the spirit within in,
from the top of your head to the bottom of your feet
joy makes one tingle like one's old lost friend.   There is joy in
the morning,
there's joy at night, there's joy in the afternoon,
there's joy in the evening.   There's joy for the moon
and more for the sun, and joy for the rain that comes in early
spring.
There is much joy at births and of birthdays that come,
but the joy of a friend is the best joy there is.
I sing for the joy of the slaves that have gone
who knew only of torment and grief that was borne.
For evil brings sadness without a glimmer of hope
and that is the cruelest that was done to you.
I sing praise to you for all the things that you have suffered*

and pray for the comfort of that pain once endured.
But with the journeys that you have made, we keep praying for a
day
when we can all be each other friendships to be made,
for friendship is a love of a strength that you showed
for in your pain you showed us how to love.
So as we gather around in this room filled with much hope and
joy,
we thank you for those journeys of yours.
We pray to keep striking down those cruelest of thoughts
for man should be ashamed of his innermost thoughts,
for sicknesses are born but take nurturing to grow,
so now we ask that they never be given even the time to be
explored,
for all of those cruel acts just stole from the lives,
of a people so proud that were afraid to cry,
but in their fear they taught us how to love,
so again we thank them for their torment and tears,
for they showed us how to live and remain more alive.
Love is not a dream neither is the hate
but love makes one laugh and feel so much joy,
so we pray that we may continue to love
and to share so that we may to continue to teach those we love.
For all those slaves of unmentionable crimes,
we thank you for your love that you've sent from time to time.
And if we ever get to feel that spirit of love,
then we'll soar like the birds that are leaving their nests.
So we will sing of the joy that awaits our world,
and we sing to the world of a joy that's once received,
for the love that's a coming like the air that we breathe.

When you look at your life growing up in this country, and how it relates to your past, your present and your future, it forces you to really think. You think about how nothing comes before it is time, that's what someone once told me, and I tell people the same, and if it didn't happen before, perhaps it wasn't supposed to happen. This is probably true to an extent; that is until you reach a time when you learn how to make things happen for you. You tell yourself to be grateful and appreciative of what has happened in your life and to enjoy it. Well, that is a bitter pill to swallow because your imagination is huge, wild and you can't help but imagine what it would be like if there had not been this hatred supreme, if there had not been this kind of incarceration, if there had not been this bondage, and more so if it had not been by the same government that once allowed all of those things to be done to your people, and now they tell you that you matter to them.

It feels like a parent that is about to give you a whipping, a beating for something that you really didn't think warranted being beat, or maybe it was for something that you didn't even do, and then they tell you that this is going to hurt them more than it's going to hurt you. You look at them with a kind of horror on your face, with a look of amazement of how could that be true when you are the one that will feel the pain, not them, that you will be the one will the marks from this whipping, not them. You are their flesh and blood so how could they do this to you? You think that how could they think or make you believe that this is going to hurt them more than it is hurting you? This would be impossible, and you try to tell them as they begin to beat your flesh. You say then don't beat me, you don't have to beat me if you love me, but they continue to beat you for they've turned a deaf ear to you just as the slave master turned a deaf ear to their father's father, or their mother's mother, and then that father turned a deaf ear to his son too. Yes, this kind of terrorism, that slave mentality had followed the Black man and Black woman from the time of slavery, and you would only understand that why they were beating you was because they never wanted this vile creature, this White man, to ever lay his hand on you and have to beat you. So what they were doing, they were doing what they never wanted him to do; they really thought that they were saving you from him. Only you would only begin to understand what had happened many years later, later when the beatings were over and you were an adult, then that's when through reading, watching TV and the like that this connection was made, and it made you feel another horror altogether. And now this same government that abused your AAPC through slavery, this same government wanted you to believe that they now cared for you too, well you had been educated much more than they would ever know, and you weren't buying this story of theirs for anything in this entire world.

I think part of you must be stunned to some degree because it only took them almost four hundred years and counting, and there is still so much more work to be done, but now there is a huge complication. There is always some complication, but this complication was brought on by the fact that your country, our country, has been attacked, and now you know it's the Whites in this country, whose needs always surpassed yours, who will be thrust to the front even more. You are now the stepchildren again, as if that had ever changed, perhaps this time you are not considered to be as ugly or less smart, but you are the stepchildren, and the White man's fears and their children must be quelled and nurtured first. A part of them knows that they've been terrorizing you for years, so they feel that you can wait, so what?

Thank God for the love that you gave to us to share, thanks for the blessing. These lessons we have learned have been from the cruelest of cruelties that have been done to man, but we had it within us to survive, so with our strength we have endured. We lost so much yet we still endured for in this loss we cried, yet continued to love for we know what it means to cherish our lives, so we lost but we loved, and we made it through, that no matter what we went through we continued to thrive, and so now we teach of how to survive. And as a people we continue to make progress by leaps and bounds each and every day.

And then there were those tough, emotionally rough days like today that I go through. Thank God that I really don't have too many of these days, they are too draining, and really rather rough. The sun was different today. What happened today, or should I say what I felt today was just rough, very tense, and an eye-opener you might say. It had a lot to do with love and how it relates to people, always expecting the best, but not necessarily getting it, you know the story, and some of you have probably been there often. Perhaps that's really not the best way to look at life, but let's face it and be real, life is, and life isn't. You don't get the best from people all the time, so why expect it? Why continue living in a fairy tale world of a fabulous imagination, no matter how great that might sound, where part of your mind can see the sun shining with a background of wonderful greenery, blue skies, ponds of ducks and geese, and children playing in the park with dogs, then playing on swings, and squirrels amongst the tree with birds flying high?

Let's begin to look at life through the eyes of say a different painter, but you know that it's really not a painter who is looking at the sun shining in a garbage dump, with smoldering decaying parts, or of alleys full of drug addicts, rapists, and streets of homeless people on filthy streets and dirty apartment complexes where there is no heat or hot water, and holes and cracks all over, where rats are running, and then let's look at that same sun shining on those people's lives. I think their sun might look quite different to them in their atmosphere of devastating gloom. When there isn't food to eat, forget about a table to put it on, there just isn't any or enough food, and you are not in any foreign country but in a land of milk and honey, a country that has wealth beyond your wildest imagination, your country, the United States of America.

Today, when speaking with a friend, I spoke of going to hide, going into my own spirit of place, something I would do as a child, somewhere that I knew that I'd be safe. I spoke of my parents and the slave mentality of my father and mother when it came to beating us as children, as something that was done for generations, like what the master had done to his slaves, which in turn caused the fathers and mothers to do the same to their children.

I now recall that I either read or saw in a movie where the slaves beat the child so that the White man wouldn't beat their child, that he had to beat the child and really beat the child to satisfy the master in order to keep the master from beating his child even worse. Oh the White man has a lot to answer for indeed. This was a kind of mental sickness that was passed from one generation to another, and it was still strong long after slavery. It took a long time for the Black man and woman to understand that this actually was slave mentality; some never even realized what had happened to them and their forefathers. The mental sickness that I am talking about here is not the White man, that is a given, but how the Black man had to become obsessed with the punishment of his own children so that they wouldn't be beat as they had been beaten by this White man. This sickness was prevalent throughout the 20th century, long after slavery. The hugging that was missing in my family and so much of the African-American families was something that was missing because the parents didn't want to show too much affection, or to become too attached to their own children for fear that they would be taken away by the master – imagine that.

Right now not a day goes by without me thinking of some of the cruelties of the White man, it's like I'm being suffocated as I try to create things that I'd like to create, but then I remember, I remember the cruelty that was done to me, done to my mother, and done to my brother. Things come back to haunt you long after you thought you'd let them go and put them to rest, and you probably did, but sometimes they re-enter your mind, resurfacing like a mist that you didn't want to see because it brought a dew that was not of growth, just spoilage.

It's amazing how things re-enter your mind, all of a sudden you remember things perhaps you put out of your mind, but now they're re-emerging. I guess that's what they called long-term memory; even people with Alzheimer's disease have it. As a child this enabled you to live in your own little world where you felt safe. This was your spirit of place, and you realize where you got your strength from because you had to, and thank God that you were given a great imagination of love and beauty, of things that you could only imagine, that is right until the day when you could make them real. No one in the world, friend, family, or foe had to know about your imagination until it was time, and when it was, well then, it would be okay, you'd gotten through the roughest part, childhood. In short this was called taking care of yourself.

Many years ago someone asked me if I knew what I wanted to be, and I really couldn't answer that then because I didn't really know where my life was leading me, and what I thought I wanted just slipped by, it didn't seem that important anymore. I didn't know what the spirit was telling me then, perhaps I wasn't as in touch with it then as now, and I had no idea what was to be extracted from me to make me remember so that I could begin creating and writing, and begin to tell some of the stories that were on my mind. A mind that I feel was very gifted, and somewhat sad too, but I knew that there was much joy coming like the dawn of the earth on my birth at springtime.

I've lived a life that I know has to change, but now I want to change it, and what I feel now enables me to spring forth and talk, smile, write and remember without turning my cheek for I am hard, not soft, I am angry, not gentle, I am cold, but yet I am not frigid, and I am so loving that I can handle those hard edges, I can sense the softness of nature, and the anger that I see is the anger of generations gone by too afraid to cry, too afraid to speak, too afraid to show love, but not frigid, for I can enjoy the cold of a wonderful frost, I can enjoy the warmth of spring of budding trees and blossoming flowers, and I can enjoy the sweat of a hot summer sun that forbids one to run, it's there, and it has become my way of enjoying those endearing moments given to me by Mother Nature.

Now I recall it being said in other writings of yesteryears that they were afraid to love for fear that their child might be taken away from them. The White man caused this fear to be passed along to other generations, and you ask me about forgiveness, ha!

Today brought me to another reality of my life, my life

without love, which can be distressful and painful, but I have food. It is very painful because I want to share, but I have clothing, I have food, and I have a table to eat off, even a tablecloth if I want to put one on. I have candles, not because I don't have light but for atmosphere, and shelter to keep me from the cold and other bad elements that are out there in those streets and alleys, and hot and cold running water, so do you see what my sun was like today?

Then as I stood here realizing that this is not the place for me, such a busy place but yet so cold, almost frigid. The atmosphere is old, there doesn't seem to be anything new or even cheerful, just old and stagnant like the air that is twice breathed in a closed-in barn waiting for a strong breeze. When I leave again, whether to go abroad like before, or perhaps when I move I will honor the freshness like with the coming of spring, and the dew that fell in the early morning hours. Oh, how I thank you for the light and lighting that shines on me – I am truly grateful.

It's a strange and very difficult time that we live in today, one that is filled with so much hatred and lies that it's suffocating its people, as if the air is really cut off from them. People mean nothing to this government; they only care about things, yes things, products that can make them richer and richer. I despise this government that we have because it refuses to take care of its people. And agencies, well, they too are despicable, for they are truly taking advantage of many workers, paying them less than that they paid when we were under another Democratic administration, an administration when this country was thriving and the people working made better wages, or at least that's the way it seemed.

11. Rude People

Jobs are hard enough to find these days, but when looking for a job, and you take your time, get dressed and go on an interview and show up on time, have a nice interview, and then the person from the agency says that they will call you as soon as they hear anything, you say to yourself great, perhaps someone will call this time. The reason that I say this time is because one doesn't want to be negative, but you've heard that time and time again, and no one ever calls. And when you call to see if anything did in fact come in, they will ask who you are, then pretend like they remember who you are, and then tell you again that they will call you again as soon as something comes in.

Well thank God I got used to people lying for rarely did anyone ever call back, or even call you back after you had gone on another job interview from the agency that you were registered with who sent you for a perspective job at one of their clients. They ask you to contact them after your interview and you do, and then they promise that they will give you a call as soon as they hear from that company, well one would be dead if they held their breath waiting for that call to come.

Disappointments come every day, so why can't they call you and let you know that the company went with someone else? Rude people get on my nerves, that's what they are, and they are also non-professional; common courtesy seem to be almost nonexistent.

On one interview, a woman told me to call her back either later in the day or first thing the next morning, so I did. A nice young man answered the phone asking who I wanted to speak to, I told him, and then he said that she was on the phone, then he was nice and asked if she was expecting my call, asking my name, and I said yes. When he returned to the phone, he said that she was busy filling an order, and that I should call back later in the day without giving me a time. People that you must depend on aren't as nice as you think they should be, not at all, so many keep you hanging, they know that you are the one that needs the work, not them. You see that respect is truly a thing of the past. This one woman kept busy and never once called me back to say that she was sorry for not getting back to me, and you know this woman had initially phoned me to have me come in for an interview. I kept phoning her until one day I stopped, but unfortunately being the one in need seems to be the lowest today. All that this means is that these agencies and companies can play games with all the potential employees, and they do.

These agencies really resemble this government of ours, for they keep you waiting, but keep in mind of course that the government is a step higher because they are taking your money and giving you nothing for it; they're sending it overseas. We're waiting on healthcare, other social programs that they continue to cut, so again this government is being rude to us, for they only have to come up with some excuses, even flimsy excuses will do, and they know that they can keep us hanging because we depend on them. They only depend on us to get elected, but that only takes a few lies to its gullible citizens, so they know that they have us by the balls, so to speak.

We also have millions of elderly citizens, and millions of minorities who are very poor, and the middle class is virtually nonexistent, so they know that they can keep us hanging because we're too miserable to really be effective. They know that some of us are hung on the late night shows, and well the others, well they've taken the drive out of us with their non-action already. So agencies are playing right along with the government, keeping us frustrated, but at the same time keeping us in dire need of their help, so they continue to control the American public like puppets. And like I said before, White people are included in this along with the minorities because you too are poor.

I'm not talking about the rich, they can always steal what they must, but you and I are different, so they continue to rob us. There comes a time when you have to count on yourself. I thought that I knew what I wanted when I came to New York many years ago, but evidently I didn't, or if I did it changed, and I was so far out there that I had to come back to me to realize what it was, so I write. What became of the sharing, something that I always wanted to do? I always wanted to share my life with that special person, but my relationships didn't last, so I guess I chose the wrong men, or I let them choose me. It's not that they didn't have anything to do with the breakups, but nonetheless, I either chose them or just let them choose me, whether it was simultaneous or not. In any case, for the most part those chosen were bizarre jealous alcoholic men, but then I too was having a problem with over drinking, especially with my seizure medication, but I just wanted so badly to be normal, and to fit in.

I've decided to take control of my life, to write and not let anybody control and/or destroy me. That's right I did say destroy; I do believe that there are people out there who just want to destroy you for any number of reasons, from your looks, from your being too happy, and the list goes on. Jealousy is a bitch; it's very much like life.

Oh my God, what a vulgar society we live in, so very different than when I was raised. I am half awake, awakening trying to get my eyes open and my fingers coordinated so that I can type, trying to get my mind to function at 2:32 a.m., Friday, February 27, 2005. Happy birthday, Grandpa, wow, what a man, what a wonderful man! He's been dead now for almost twenty-one years. In remembering him, one thing that I knew he had was pride, and plenty of common sense. He had a saying: "T'ain't nothing happening today that ain't already happened." In looking at what's going on today and seeing how disillusioned this country is, their beliefs, and their so-called non-beliefs, he was right.

What a dream world, one that's filled with a reality that resembles little ginger men, and of little cricket-like men walking upside down while trying to make like they are for real. Hypocrisy, eat this, don't eat that, say this, wear this, kiss this, touch this or touch it this way, look at this, look at that, sleep with that, play this and play that, and all this make this country into one of the biggest hypocritical societies in the world, a place that we call the United States of America, a name synonymous with what's big and overdone, non-caring and arrogance.

It can be okay to eat this "if", or okay to say this "if", okay to wear this "if", and okay to kiss this "if", to touch this "if", to kiss this way "if", to look this way "if", to sleep this way "if", to play this way "if", all so long as you are part of one society that has the power to pay whatever they want to if. There are so many ifs in our society. You can sleep with your man, woman, dog or cat and anything else you want to as long as you come from the cream of the crop of society that has money and make those laws to keep your fetishes going. So long as you give enough money, basically you can say and do anything in this country that you want without those annoying ifs that the poor and middle class have. Telling lies, lies, that's what so much of this society is doing, they're either lying or swearing, cursing at their kids, and their kids are cursing at them, a truly different vulgar society we live in today, vile and offensive, no respect for anything, not yourself, not your mother or father – did I say something wrong?

If the wrong person is caught doing the nasty with another man and doesn't have enough pull, i.e. money and or political pull to keep it out of the papers, well, you know the story, he's screwed. But if it's a man with immense wealth, who has political ties, and goes to church, or for that matter be it a priest in a gown, or "dress" as my friend calls it, then it's all right. What a society, such hypocrites are they. We have done more wrong in the name of who we are, and sometimes substitute God's name in there somewhere, but because of the immense money made, and the money a select few have in this country, we have become those little ginger men and little cricket-like men walking upside down while trying to make like they are for real. You get the picture – we're living in a world of fantasy.

Our society takes so many drugs that our kids have gone and started murdering Mommy and Daddy, their friends, classmates, and playmates because they don't know what's real anymore, if they do they're so high that they're barely able to tell – they really don't know. And the way kids talk to their parents and parents talk to their kids using the foulest of language, wondering where their child heard theirs from, one fouler than the next, something that one was more accustomed to hearing from truck drivers, sailors and prostitutes, it's unreal, but yet it's real.

I once heard this nice-looking well-dressed Black woman yelling at her son in McDonald's, asking him where he heard that "Goddamn fucking language", and who told him that he could use that "fucking language", and that she didn't raise him to use that damned language, and that she would beat the "Goddamn shit out of him" for using that language, and that she never gave him permission to use that "damned" language, she raised him better than to use that "fucking language, ". She went on and on until the people in McDonald's kept staring at her as if she had just lost her mind, until she caught herself and what she was saying. Some just laughed for she was using this vile, this most inappropriate language in a restaurant no less, but she had the audacity to ask her son where he heard this language. Well, we know where he heard it, Mommy had a mouth like two truck drivers, a sailor and a prostitute all rolled into one, and that was about fourteen years ago, so it's only gotten worse.

Evidently love has been squashed out of lives like bullets fired in the Iraqi streets, or that were once fired on the Mississippi streets or the streets of Alabama, the streets of Atlanta and Tennessee, of Watts, of Philadelphia, South Carolina, and Detroit, of Chicago, Boston and LA, Albany, Bridgeport, Dallas and New York, Miami, North Carolina, Washington, D.C. just to name a few, and bullets flying in those drive-by shootings, and all because of what? So many are because of the drugs that have infiltrated our cities, but don't forget about those that were done because of prejudices.

Today, you don't want to give anyone the rights that you have, or the simple right to love if it's not your way. You still want to be God, but He's still around and never asked that you interfere with His work. You have done far too much on your own as it is, He even gave you His son, but you murdered Him too, so for once stay out of His plan, for He needs no help from a people like you. You see this is a funny and cruel society, it's a crying shame, they can laugh at you or spit in your face, or cut your throat before they would take the time to discover who you are and what you want, what you need or why you want or need any of it. Believe what you want, non-caring, that's what it is. Would you believe your mother, your father, or your best friend if they made you suffer, raped and murdered your friends and neighbors, but told you that they did so because they thought it was in your best interest? You don't allow all of the things to happen that you have accused other people or governments of doing, like those dictators in those other countries; you don't allow this to happen in your country if you care for someone, if you love someone. And you definitely wouldn't be murdering another country of people, telling people here that you're doing so for them.

This country is like the little ginger men and little cricket-like men walking upside down while trying to make like they are for real. It's got to be, no man or woman in their right mind would allow such hypocrisy, such non-lovingness, if there is such a word, to keep on going on, they wouldn't allow this if they really cared. For what does it matter if a man sleeps with another man or if he sleeps with a woman? Be concerned about what's happening in your own front yard, your own backyard, not anyone else's. Be concerned, help feed someone, be concerned, help clothe someone, be concerned, help someone to secure a job so that they can maintain a roof over their head and food on their table. They're not asking you to love them; you've proven to them already that you can't do that. Here in this country alone, you have been raping, robbing, stabbing, torturing, and murdering people for hundreds of years, and because a man loves another man and they want to get married, you get so bent out of shape that you want to change the constitution – get out of here!

You should have gone back and taken a look at that constitution to make sure the African-American People of Color were included in everything and made us as inclusive as you Whites instead of trying to change the constitution because you think God must have made some kind of mistake. This country is shamelessly ridiculous. Raping little boys in church, sodomizing children, and you're now just beginning to uncover those sins of the fathers, no pun intended, but yes fathers – yours not mine. 10,667 cases of sexual abuse from 1950 through 2002 in the Catholic Church alone, and over $840,000,000.00 have been paid out since the 1950s.

http://www.betnahrain.org/bbs/index.pl/noframes/read/23525
http://www.democraticunderground.com/discuss/duboard.php?az=view_all&address=104x3144928
http://formercatholicsforchrist.yuku.com/topic/3788
http://www.usmessageboard.com/religion-and-ethics/25121-catholic-church-demands-celibacy-for-gays-too.html
http://books.google.com/books?ct=result&q=Catholic+Church,+$840,000,000&btnG=Search+Books

And now you have a problem about whom we sleep with, and the fact that yes, I want to share my life with someone that I love, for some reason that disturbs you. We want equal rights and we deserve them. You can love your man, and you can love your woman, but when you're honest and not hypocritical about the real person whom you love and want to show it, this country doesn't want you to do that, and why because they have really messed up when it comes to loving anyone or anything.

It was okay for them to rape and sodomize my people in slavery, and after slavery in the prisons, even today. It was okay for you to hang, tar and feather my people when you didn't like the way they looked at you. It was okay for you to castrate our men and sterilize our women, experimenting with us, making us a cruel experiment, hanging someone and all of the other atrocities that you committed, and only God knows what else, and you have a problem with men sleeping with men, and women sleeping with women. Men who are kind, that are gentle, protecting our country, men working in the highest offices in this land, and probably in the office next to you, but men who aren't hurting anyone, and you have a problem with this?

If It's Done Out of Love

If it's done out of love, then why should anyone care?
For what I need and what you need are just two worlds apart,
so all you have to do is try and understand, that if I haven't judged
you for everything you think, then why should you now judge me
because of the way I think? There comes a time when people should

have some respect even though they haven't used it, or perhaps
they just forgot. In any case you should remember when we
were
growing up, a time when you loved us oh so much then,
or was that just pretending or were you really our friends?
And if you really were a friend of ours, then please be one right
now,
and try to be accepting of my life that's not so different than
yours right now,
for in our relationships, there's joy, there's laughter and
friendship too,
not saying that there's no hardships because they do come too,
but that joy and friendship is based on a real love we share,
that when we were growing up you once shared with us too,
so don't be hypocritical now as this nation is with us,
for this is our time of need, and even if we differ,
we should still be the same to you, for we are the children that
God gave to you,
and if you believe in anything today, believe that God knew what
He was doing when He created you and me.

They have no idea what real love is all about, they'd rather resemble little ginger men and little cricket-like men walking upside down while trying to make like they are for real. Leave things which you know nothing about alone and let them be. *Love is the most precious thing in the world, it's beautiful, and then there's the laughter.* You can't teach it because you don't really know what it means. The church can't teach it either, they're still destroying our kids while bringing in beaucoup dollars, dollars that you are still giving them, and this is mega millions every year under the guise of love and Christianity for what they've done to your kids. Hell, men wore skirts long before women; they are still wearing their kilts in Scotland, they used to fight in them, as did the Egyptians. In the name of love, I can tell you, probably show you, perhaps I should be the teacher. Yes, America messed up a very long time ago, and she still refuses to make it right, even after hundreds of years of cries.

Being unafraid to give, that's what we must become. Being unafraid to love, that's what I must be.

When love can make you cry and laugh at the same time, then you know it must be real. To be able to cry about something, and to laugh about something right after is truly a joy that everyone should experience at least once.

12. Passion

Passion, it's all about passion, passion, and more passion, passion to live, passion to love and passion to write, passion to work, and passion to just be. Passion to think, to laugh, to smile, passion to speak, to look, to touch and passion to feel. Oh how I love this wonderful, this marvelous, this sometimes fragrant, but all so gentle passion. Passion to see, to hear, to listen, to read, to eat, and passion that makes me hungry as I thirst, eat and drink. Passion to smell the good earth, for it is good when left alone. God's work is truly wonderful, marvelous, and it is the best. Passion to see, oh look at those wonderful trees, mountains, birds, cats, dogs, snakes, flowers, butterflies, dirt, grass, rivers, oceans, and those wonderful passionate clouds that bring the passionate rain, for passionate sweet water. That passionate air that we breathe every day, less we die, the passionate sun that shines to help us all to grow in so many ways, plus that passion to brighten our spirits. The passionate moon that rises, changing until it finally becomes full, changing us in ways that we cannot explain, imagine or ignore, for love or for money, and that passionate sex. That moon glow strengthens our spirit so passionately, and yes it makes us yearn,

yearn for passionate, wonderful, stimulating sex. I do need this passion, and for reasons that I really don't know, it's been failing me for too long, or perhaps it's me that has been failing to realize my passion, or my truest passion...Passion is my joie de la vie. I need passion in my life; it makes me feel so alive, so full of life, and this passion has faded in me so much since of 2002. I need and want to be happy, I need and want to share, I need and want to love, yes love, real love exposed. Love is so precious, it is the most precious thing in the world. It's beautiful, it's charming, it's warm, gentle, and oh so soothing. It's like a fresh snowflake melting on you face, it's like a fragrant gardenia that blossoms over and over, sending such a fragrant enticing smell that enhances your spirit, that makes you shiver, and finally if there is a finality in passion, it is the love which is truly like a mother, her look, her touch ever so nurturing, talking to you, telling you everything will be all right, that you are good, that you are beautiful, and then there's that wonderful laughter, oh so joyful. Oh what passion brings, it can warm you on a cold evening and cool you on the hottest summer day, what a feeling. It can tingle the cockles of your mind.

I don't hate, but I do despise. There are reasons which have been seen, reasons for which there is really no excuse for anyone to steal that which is yours, especially the passion. We are strong caring people but we can be gentle, we have much bitterness inside, but we can be soft, and oh we can be like ice, but preferring to be a warm ocean for love is something that comes oh so naturally to us. We want our passion back. Oh, United States of America, give us back our passion, you've stolen enough, and more than enough you have taken. You've shown us over the years that you really don't care, but we care. Give us this passion back for it is ours. Now you say that you do care and want that we believe you, so if this is true, and if you do really care, then give this passion back for it is ours. Peace is what we need, peace, and love, and laughter, bring it back, bring it back, give it back for it is right.

Having grown up in this country, the realities that faced me made me feel as if I were in a dream world, but realistically put, I was in a state of shock for so much of my life. Looking back on my life, I realize that others' hopes and dreams were not for me, they were not designed for my people, for we weren't considered a whole people. I've always been a person that is able to retreat back into myself, for in me, I am able to find comfort and strength and see more clearly. In myself is a spirit of place so new and so old that it is my well from which I draw my strength. It's my water that God gave me to comfort me, it is my River Nile that can either be rough or smooth, it is my true spirit of place, and though I can share other spirit of places and have, this spirit of place no one really knows except the good Lord and me. You might ask if I want to share it, and my answer would be not really. You might ask why? Simply because you usually strike down that which you don't understand or refuse to understand. I feel that this country has had hundreds of years to understand, hundreds of years to do better, and it really hasn't, so why should I share that which is truly the essence of me? Like I told someone years ago when they asked me who I was, I plainly told them that I am me. I am me, and that suits me fine, they still wonder if I'm sure, but that's fine, I am still me.

You see there are things that you learn as you live, and one learns more if you are fortunate enough to grow older, and if you are willing to open your mind, your heart and be willing to be a little more receptive. Some things change, others remain unchanged and these things might be a little disturbing, but one has to learn how to journey around them. Look at history, and if you were fortunate to be born Black, you will probably understand just what I'm talking about. One might say that statement sounds very ominous, but being born Black, with all of the struggle that we faced and still face, has taught us lessons that we probably could have never learned had it not been for some of these things.

This society treats dogs, cats and other pets better than other human beings; just look at what is going on and how pets are treated. Look at the way animals are fed, and then take a look at how they are groomed, and what care they are given when they become ill, or where they stay when their masters go on a trip or vacation where their pets aren't allowed go. Why there are beautiful shelters where these animals are sent for the best care. But then look at the way children are treated, and tell me that you love your children. So many of you don't even believe your children when they tell you something, your dogs and cats can't talk, but you rush them off to the vet and feed them the finest of foods, but some of you, if your child's complaint doesn't sound real enough to you, you'll tell them to stop complaining and you will go on your merry little way watching some TV series that is not of any importance until your child becomes feverish. Then you'll get excited and start calling or rush them to the emergency, and you'll be asking them why they didn't tell you before. Your children can only tell you but so much, after all, they are children, but your pets can't even talk, and you whisk them off to the vet for the most minor of incidents.

I don't ever want to let wisdom pass me by, neither do I want to ever let love pass me by. Love is life, it's precious and adorning, it's a crown rich and poor alike can wear and be proud, for love is, and it knows no boundaries – none. Love encompasses all of us, just allow yourself to feel, to feel the spirit and its warmth, and if you open up, it will take hold of you, if you just succumb to it. *"Love is the most precious thing in the world, and then there's the laughter"*!*!*Ø

What does my passion mean to me, or to put it another way, what is passion?

Learning is one of the most fascinating things that one can accomplish, it's a task, but just think of all that can be amassed if you just listen to others when they speak to you – listen, not just hear them, and listen to their thoughts. I want you to listen to beautiful thoughts, thoughts that make you laugh and smile, wonderful thoughts that make the heart want to comfort another heart, not destroy another heart or another person, or life, or a city, or a country, or dog, or cat, or church or synagogue or mosque or anything that is held sacred, whether you understand it or not. No destruction, none, but only destroy that which is destroying, and make it complete. Just remember that nothing is complete, only love, so let love invade all of us to be completely loving, and in love so we won't feel the need to destroy anything, except the destroyer that is lying, cheating, hurting and killing you, your child, your mother, your sister, your brother, your father, your friends and your lover. Help destroy the destroyer, bring your spirit to fight the fight that only the spirit knows how to fight.

Only the spirit knows how to take care of his children, only the spirit knows how to really love for HE/SHE is love supreme, so listen to the spirit. Listen to the spirit when it says take heed because it means just that – take heed. The spirit is not just love supreme, but of course it is, the spirit is that wonderful blessing that Grandma, that Grandpa, all the great-grandparents have taught us, it reigns supreme, and in reigning supreme it is called common sense. Funny thing, not all of us possess common sense – we don't. You can't expect others to utilize that which they don't have, and that's one of the biggest problems facing this country; beside the arrogance, the greed, and the hypocrisy of this country, common sense is lacking.

I bet you think these politicians possess the quality of common sense – wrong. They are the children, the old children that need to take instruction from the old wise people that have gone before, the old wise men, women and children that have never hurt anyone. They need to take instruction, and they who remain arrogant need to be put out to pasture in the fields where they will have to learn how to truly do for themselves, yes, put them in the wild. Let the wild be taken care of by the wild. Change will then come, and then harmony will be able to begin.

For me this journey started many years ago, but this particular part of the journey came to mind simply by feeling different. I was born here, yet I felt different, I was raised here, yet I felt different, I went to school here, yet still I felt different, and I worked here, but I still felt different because you made me feel different. That's not a good quality that you possess, for it's nothing that you should feel proud of. Having lived, experienced and as one continues to live, experience and observe, I have noticed that I really felt out of place here, out of place in this, my own country where I was born, that's not the way that it's suppose to be. Asking myself several questions and trying to understand this, I began thinking, and then I realized that this wasn't anything that I'd done, it wasn't anything that I'd said, so why did I feel so uncomfortable here? As I began to think, as my mind opened up and my thoughts became much more serious, I wanted to understand this feeling.

Like watching a flower or a tree grow, you want to know more about that flower or that tree, you're fascinating about how something can grow and blossom if you just leave it alone. You leave it alone unless you see that it's getting dry and needs a little water, so you make sure that it has water, other than that you leave it alone, and nature takes care of it. You watch these wonderful things grow living and dying, and making it through each day, week, month, from season to season. You see how nature protects them, and you see how the flowers come back because they were left alone and not uprooted. You see the trees getting bigger and stronger for they have a much longer life span than these humble little flowers. Again nature has provided for them and no one has uprooted them, no one has disturbed them. Then one begins to understand how simple life can be without disturbances.

We look at the insects such as bees, and we begin to understand their connection with those flowers, and how year after year they pollinate and do their thing, providing honey from the nectar of those flowers, but never destroying the beauty. No one bothers them, so they flourish year after year, and each year they work in harmony with each other again.

Now we begin looking at animals and perhaps we study them and we understand how God's creatures live together, protect each other and basically only destroy in order to survive. And if man leaves them alone, they too live much much longer.

Now comes the evolution of when you start looking into your own life, and this marvelous splendid human being like yourself, who is an amazing creature, and you begin to laugh a little, cry a little, and then cry a whole lot more when you look at the human race of which you're a part, but in particular your own people, the Black people here in the United States of

America. As you begin to cry you realize that unlike the flowers, unlike the trees, unlike the insects, and unlike the animals, your race of people, the Black race from Africa, weren't left alone. We were disturbed, we were uprooted, we were not left alone to grow and flourish amongst our own. No something much worse happened, something that became one of the worst acts of man's inhumanity to man happened, and that was just the beginning. Only it didn't just happen, someone caused it to happen, it was you that caused it, it was this country, the United States of America, who wanted slaves to do their work, who wanted slaves to be their toys, who wanted slaves to be their whores, and who wanted slaves to be their dogs.

Now look at how plants and flowers grow and show their love to you, they grow without sunlight or any light that is natural, and still you destroy that which gives you so much, and you give them so little, their fathers and mothers, you know those beautiful trees. They beautify our offices so much even under the coldest and most frigid tongues of human beings, yet they smile for you every day and don't ask much from you at all. Yet you slaughter those trees for no real reason at all, and then get angry when there isn't enough. Learn the humility from your plants, love them and care for them the way they care for all of us.

Disturbances are such a plague, and that began to gnaw at my spirit. It became an irritant, and now I have to finally come to terms with it and relate it to others. Beginning to realize all these things, reality came to me like a swift kick in the mouth, and when that happened to me, this told me that this country will call you what they want, that is if you let them, so much rudeness and so much ignorance. This is a common trait when people don't have an understanding of something or someone, or even care to understand. And also this country found out that we Black people were very intelligent, and that scared them – it still does. You see today we are not called "Colored People" or "Negroes", but Black, African-American People of Color, but if we don't keep our eyes and ears open, you might try calling us something else, but it is our decision of what we will be called, not yours, not theirs. So my people, be careful, be very careful of what names you call each other, for one day soon because of your own mouths and those words that you use, that too will come back to you.

Sometimes I think this country is blind, for they only see what they want to when it comes to my people. As stated earlier, they see only what they want, but we're saying that the way we're seen matters because we are people, a very unique people, and it is our decision to make sure that you take notice – we refuse to allow you deny to us that.

You can play ignorant or remain in denial on other things, but not when it comes to the things that make us unique. For instance, our skin color, you want to remain totally blind there, but it wasn't our men who raped your women, but your men who raped our Black women, so now you will look and identify what you see, after all you need to take a good look at what you caused. We've taken control of our lives, and as I am taking control of mine, it is we who will have the final say. You see my views are strong, some may not agree with them, but they are mine nonetheless; they came to me in an honest fashion.

When looking at this country and Christianity and the so-called White Christian in this country, or should I say the White Christian as it pertains to our political structure within this government, my mind is really confused. Having been raised in a strict Methodist family tradition, what I was taught as a churchgoer who later became a Christian was good vs. evil. What was good was taught by examples put forth in the Bible and out of the Bible, and what was evil was also shown in the Bible and out of it, and in our daily lives. Amazing as it might seem, I neither read anything that would make our government a Christian nation by its thoughts, words or deeds. What I see is that Christianity is being used as a tool to front what this nation is doing, in much the same way that a prostitute uses a john, and the way they are using this tool to cover up things is a deadly obsession that I fear will cost them later on as it is costing them now. A prime example is the lie they told the American people and to the world about the weapons of mass destruction.

It is quite amazing that some of these same people, some who are in the very government that is running this country, your elected officials, swear that they believe in God and are Christians, but when we look at their actions, it looks as though they must feel that being a Christian is okay part-time at best. They must because look at the way they act when they are governing this country, when they are deciding who will have food, who will have jobs, who will have shelter, who will have clothing, and who will have medicine, and who will vote. They are governing us, the people, and what they are showing us is definitely not Christian-like, not even part-time Christian-like. They are seen as world leaders that are supposed to be setting good examples, not with a preemptive strike on a country and its people, not by fighting, murdering, stealing and destroying others, things like that don't even resemble Christianity. So if it is Christianity as a part-time thing, it must be when they are sleeping, like some of the people that you probably have met or know from your own realm of acquaintances.

It seems that politics and religion don't go together, or to put it more precisely that they don't want religion in their politics, and why because they don't really want to have to be good people. Now I understand why they wanted to separate religion and politics, they didn't want the religion hanging over them, guiding them. They wanted to still be able to be nasty, to still be prejudiced, to be discriminatory, to be able to destroy, and to be able to annihilate people and other countries at will. But you know God does not work that way, God created the entire world, the entire universe, and He does not play that way, you either believe in God in entirely or you don't believe in Him at all. Whether you want it, whether you like it or not, God is a part of all things. You either follow His rules in their entirety or you don't at all. It is not up to you to decide when you're going to obey God, it doesn't work that way, so for those who think that while they're in politics they really are not governed by God, they're wrong, everything in this universe, even the most infinitesimal part, is governed by the Creator. So the politics is included, it's how you are respecting your neighbors, other human beings, how you are respecting this good earth or if you are not respecting at all, this is how you either show glory to God or not, you don't make the rules, God makes the rules, so it's up to you to play by the rules, so if you say no, just beware when God says no.

This country has the biggest pair of brass balls that I could ever imagine, bigger than fifty million bulls times two. You might say, "Hey that's some big, huge, humungous balls," and I agree. It all has to do with mathematics, when you multiply all of those sins which are great, then the multiplication of those wrongs are enhanced, and then multiplying those dastardly deeds, and the evil wicked ways, then adding those vehement lies, and when those things being done are done in the name of Christianity, well then everything really gets magnified, and then pretending to be a God-fearing country, well that really takes the cake. It's like they must think that God is really stupid. To start with, they came to this country for religious freedom, as least that's what I was taught, and when they arrived the Indians, whose homeland this was, provided them with comfort. They taught them how to take care of this land, grow and harvest their crops, how to cultivate the soil, how to nurture it so that they could grow food. Now one would think that good deeds would in turn cause other goods deed from those foreigners, but unlike the goodness that is shown in the Bible, these same foreigners, the White man, decided that they wanted something that wasn't theirs, this land, so they began to manipulate, rob, steal and murder those good people.

In doing so they steadfastly said that they were Christians, much in the same way they do today. Amazing, shocking, horridly amazing, wouldn't you agree? After doing that and scouring this land with their evil ways, they found that they needed help, so what did they do? Well, they decided to go and get something else that wasn't theirs. After deciding upon where to go, they went to Africa, the land of Black kings and Black queens that were rich beyond their wildest imagination. Once they got there, they decided that they could buy under false pretenses, so they entered the slave market, but when they couldn't get exactly what they wanted, or the price was too high, they began stealing these strong, beautiful African people of color. They also decided that these beautiful people needed the White man's religion, Christianity, and they decided that who better to teach them but them. You see the White man needed a people that they could enslave so that they could make them do exactly what they wanted them to do, things that they wouldn't have to do for themselves. They wanted a people to be subservient to them in every way; each of them wanted to be a king and a queen here in America, something that they left in Great Britain, where they were judged and made to obey.

You might ask, why did they choose these people? Well, they chose them because they were strong people, and though jealous of their strength and beauty, in chains they knew that they could control and would be able to manipulate them. Again they tried to convince themselves that they really came to this country under the guise of religious freedom, and they just needed some help, so what if they enslaved someone, they would not be the first, for that was in the Bible. You see, when they read the Bible, they read what they wanted to, leaving out that which would make them out to be the evildoer, much in the same way that people do today. When they bought or stole these magnificent people, a horror began that has never been equaled. Torture, murder and rape, just to name a few things that they did to my beautiful loving people who did them no harm.

"My country tis of thee sweet land of lib..." and they hung them from trees. "My country tis of thee sweet land of ..." and they whipped them at will. "My country tis of..." oh, they raped our women. "My country tis of thee sweet land of..." and they raped our men too. "My country tis of..." and they stole our children. "My country tis..." and they set our churches on fire, burning our homes, the men, women, and the children. "My country tis of..." and they brought the dogs in to attack us. "My country tis of..." and they shot us, and they turned the fire hoses on us like we were wild animals. "My country tis of..." and then they chained us to trees where they beat us some more. "My country tis..." and they peed on us just like dogs would do. "My country tis of..." and wild as animals they tarred and feather us too.

Who are the wild animals, who are the violent ones I ask?

We marched in peace, and we sang, who are the savages I ask? We prayed as we marched.

"My country tis of thee..." and they set fire to our lawns, our homes with their crosses, and we continued to sing and pray, and they claimed that they were Christians. "My country tis of...." and they refused to serve us food in their restaurants. "My country tis of..." and they refused lodging when we were tired and sleepy. "My country tis of..." and they refused us medical treatment at their hospitals, and at these same hospitals they sterilized our women. "My country tis of..." and they refused to allow us to use the bathrooms, we had to defecate in streets and then because we had nowhere to go, and the streets were dirtier now, they made us wear it, and pick it up with our bare hands. "My country tis of thee sw..." and they refused to allow us to drink from the same water fountain, even if the ones that they marked colored were not working and the ones marked White were working, and we paid our taxes. "My country tis of..." and they made us sit upstairs in the balcony of the movie houses. "My country tis of th..." and they refused to let us sit in the front of the bus, that is until Rosa Parks was tired one day and refused to move to the back, God bless her, and boycotts came after. "My country tis of th..." and we couldn't marry their women or their men, and their women and men couldn't marry our men and women. "My country tis of th..." and they drafted our men into their armed services, some of us joined, but they refused to give us equal treatment even there, even though we too were protecting our country. "My country tis of..." you see they even segregated us in the armed forces, but put us on the front lines so that we would be a shield for them, so that we would die first. "My country tis of..." and when the war was over people were free in other countries, we lost our lives and limbs, but they were free, but what happened to us, what happened to us? We had fought so other people could be free, freedom, freedom, yet we were not free in our own country. "My country tis of..." yes we were wounded and died in their wars, but we still didn't have freedom. You might say we were in a different kind of slavery, or the same. "My country tis of..." we were not free, we were not free, we are not free, not in this country. "My country tis of th..." America is not a just country. "My country tis of..." America is not a land of equal opportunity for us. "My country tis of th..." is still the same.

The songwriter lied, and America is still lying. In the so-called greatness of America, America is still lying; they don't know how to tell the truth. This country called the United States of America that still refuses to tell the truth to its people. "My country tis of..." what? You tell me. They have burned our homes, our churches, schools and businesses, so you tell me; they have raped our women, men and children, so you tell me. So tell me, who are the Christians, and who are the honorable men, women and children? You tell me, you tell me... I will tell you God doesn't like ugly; He never has and never will.

So you claim to be Christians, and have claimed this for years, but we say, I say, that you don't know how to be a Christian for you don't know how to live, you have no idea of how to treat people, and you don't know anything about how to love your fellow men and women. When you flunk all of the tests involved in human kindness, you flunk at being a Christian, so accept the fact that you are still the barbaric people that continue robbing, stealing and murdering just because you want it all, and God didn't give all that you thought you should have. You defy God, you spite God, you think that it must be a mistake when He denies you something, you who want it all, you who have spoiled yourself, your children, and your children's children into talking yourself into believing that you must have anything that you want. Shame on you, shame on America that could be ever so beautiful! A shameless country needs all the help that it can get, God Bless America!

I feel as if I have eaten something poisonous that I need to regurgitate and am in need of an anti-venom serum, but there isn't any. I feel that I have eaten too much of the wrong food, and that it hasn't agreed with me, and I feel that this country has made me sick and has constipated me, and I really need to take a long crap. I feel like I've been cheated, and like it was done on purpose. In this country, how we hoped, how we dreamed, how we sacrificed, but no one seemed to care. "My country tis oh sweet land..." but not for me, not for me, for me it seems like I was born in the wrong country.

Thinking on the whole situation about the apology which has still not been given by the United States of America to the African-American People of Color, and it really doesn't look as though one is forthcoming any time soon, your mind begins to wonder. Could it be possible that perhaps they, meaning White people, think that they are exempt or should be exempt from being included in the process when it comes to an apology to the African-American People of Color? Another thing that comes to mind is how does this country ever think that the African-American People of Color will ever trust anything that they say, trust the fact that this country cares for them in any way if they are first not even willing to extend this long overdue apology and admission of their guilt?" An olive branch must be extended to the Black race that did you no harm; it was you that did unspeakable harm to the Black race. When so much harm has been done by this nation, it is this nation that must first take the responsibility and show that this government will no longer do harm to the African-American People of Color before any trust can ever be established. This government must be stark raving mad if they think that we'll trust them if they are not even willing to be responsive to that most crucial need.

The first question in particular came to mind since it's been well of over one hundred and thirty-five years since the abolition of slavery, and nothing has been paid to the African-American People of Color, and no apology has been made. It would seem that even the most mentally challenged people could and would have apologized by now. The reason that I am putting this forth is because when one is dealing with an arrogant government and a country that is made up of predominantly White people; one only knows what to expect. I've lived in this country all my life; I am fifty-five now, soon to be fifty-six, and from what I see, the people and the hierarchy involved in this country don't really set my heart afire. This nation has never apologized before; rather they have refused to admit that slavery in this country was a cruel and usual treatment, and that it was a crime against humanity. For this reason, in trying to figure out the why, and because it puzzled me greatly, that's when I began thinking, could I be naïve when it comes to thinking this, that they must know that it is them that need to apologize, it was them, it was their grandparents and great-grandparents, not mine?

They are the ones that set the holidays and made their founding father George Washington's birthday a national holiday for the American people to celebrate, not the African-American People of Color. Personally, I wouldn't have a holiday for a man who was the owner of slaves, who was part of a system that condoned slavery, that condoned the torture, and total discrimination of African-American People of Color, I wouldn't have it. So in their arrogance, is it possible that they would think they shouldn't be included? Besides the slavery issue of early America, there is also the issues that continue to allow this country of America to keep abusing the African-American People of Color long after slavery, so even though slavery was "abolished", look at what kept happening in the south long after slavery, even with the Civil Rights movement of the fifties, sixties and seventies, and the north didn't have clean hands either, so basically it was the entire country.

Let me say simply that I know they, the White people of this country, should be included, rather than to simply say they should. The reason that I know they should be included is, like I said, it was their forefathers, and the way I look at it is that if one is going to celebrate the names that they have in history, be it White, Black, Mexican or American Indian, and bring it to the American people to be celebrated, then the people should know everything that there is to know about said person or persons. The government should make sure that everything is disclosed so that their citizens can make up their minds after all of the facts are made known. All of the citizens pay taxes, and thus they all should be given full disclosure of said people and/or matters. Let the entire history of that person be known, for it is this country's intention that the people should be celebrating this person, they're celebrating the history of the entire person. In instances when people are celebrating people, they should know exactly who they're celebrating, and if they choose to celebrate that person, after all, this is a country that is supposed to be free.

After disclosing everything about this person, they can continue to celebrate these names like Washington, but only if this government, after making a full disclosure, disavows and censures the things that he stood for in writing, such as slavery because he did own slaves, and as stated earlier, it's even purported that he sold slaves for rum because he did drink, and he liked his rum.

The White people need to recognize that it was their grandfathers, great-grandfathers, and great-great-grandfathers, that it was their forefathers. They were only the African-American People of Color's forefathers by force only when they had "quote unquote" raped our great-grandmothers. Yes, whether you want to believe that or not, the forefathers of this country did that, some of history's dirty laundry just came out, and who knows how much more will be exposed. Now guess what, George Washington slept with a woman of color, his relatives started coming forth, and so did Thomas Jefferson, so surprise! American people who think that your families are all White, your so-called Christian forefathers did the nasty with more than one woman, and this included women of color. These so-called great White icons were not so wonderful, you really need to think twice and need to put into perspective what these men did to the African-American People of Color, and yes, you need to apologize for the actions of those great-grandfathers and great-great-grandfathers who forced themselves on those Black women. As far as I'm concerned, they too are responsible for stealing, raping those women, for stealing their virginity, and for soiling them. They must come to realize that if they're going to be proud of these people in history, that they must know the actions of these people, for these acts were not Godly, but barbaric, and they were definitely not consecrated by God. Therefore, if this government continues to refuse to give such an apology and admit to these crimes, then that means that even today they're still sanctioning the things that were done in the time of slavery.

13. Remembering Slavery, White Man's Cruelty, Stolen Children

Remembering some issues and remembering slavery, there is much that one can speak of when it comes to the abject cruelty that the White man caused the Africans that they stole and purchased from Africa. What inhumanity, and what terror they caused to such a peaceful, wonderful, strong and beautiful people who did no harm to them is more than shameful. The White man has always wanted to rule the world, and if you look at his history, his history will verify how barbaric, violent and dangerously mischievous the White man can be. One can't help but be apprehensive and fearful of this man because his pattern shown has not displayed him to be one of the most peace loving of all of the human beings on this wonderful earth, this beautiful world that God created. His greed precedes him, and his main objective has been to divide and conquer and take what he wanted from others. The only way that he's been able to do this is by creating things that are more dangerous and more destructive than his fellow human beings, and so far that hasn't really been a problem because his mind seems geared toward annihilation.

When remembering the issue of slavery in the United States, one can't help but remember how utterly cruel the White man became when dealing with the African slaves, the darker-skinned people that he bought and stole. He was a monster, nastier and dirtier than these beautiful people could ever have imagined him to be. When you think about that today and all the love or so-called love that's supposed to be expressed by this country towards its citizens in the United States of America to its White, Black and Hispanic cultures, and all the others that are in between, and how they supposedly care about us, I can't help but look back in anger. There is a reason that I must look back because in all of this time, there has been no apology ever made to the African-American People of Color here in this country. There was a formal apology to the Japanese, but not to the African-American People of Color, the Black people here in the United States, and like I said before, that still irks me. It angers me a great deal, but what really angers me, and sends chills down my spine is the abject treatment of these slaves, these people, these human beings, my brothers and sisters.

When I look at the years of difference of what was done to the Japanese, what was done to the Blacks and look at how long it took this country to apologize to the Japanese, and then compare the time when slavery ended to the time of the bombing of Hiroshima and Nagasaki, I really get infuriated because it only took a few short years before this country apologized to Japan. However, after over one hundred and thirty-five years, the African-American People of Color have never received an apology. You are probably saying we have read this already, and you have, but still after all that time we wait, and in telling you about this wait, it becomes necessary to make it crystal clear as to what happened in this time of American history.

It's been said that America's darkest hour is the slave issue, but I wonder because the African-American People of Color cannot move on like the Japanese. You see after that apology was made to them, that was like a little closure, but we still don't have any closure. What America did to Japan was done in a very short time, but what America did to the Black man was done over a much greater time span, over two hundred years before the abolition of slavery. Now you are probably saying, "Wow, I didn't realize it was that long. Well, the years keep on coming just like an unwanted birthday does for some of you that are conscious about your age – quite amazing, isn't it? When you thought that the slaves couldn't be treated any worse, you heard or read of something worse that the White man had done to them. It was as if he was in some kind of competition of how cruel he could be to these people, and maybe there was some sort of competition that was devised between the various slave owners, I don't really know. All that I do know is that it was evil, sick and it hurt, it maimed, and it killed, and mentally it left such an imprint in the minds of all those who survived that it continued to linger on for generations to come. This hurt, this pain, this anguish, this self-doubt, this sorrow, and this abuse was passed on to the children, that slave treatment was so harsh, and so violent that it continues to terrorize many of the African-American People of Color even today.

I want you to look at the families in this country today, really take a good look at your family with the mother, father and the wonderful children, who are loving, tender and seem like a wonderful family that is growing together, and who seem to share in their love for one another in respectful ways. Then I want you to imagine having your own child, or children if there are more than one, imagine them being taken from you, not by a

193

kidnapper that you read about in the papers today, but by a master who has total dominion over you, as the White man had over his slaves. Can you imagine ever having your own child, a child not an adult stolen from you because this master could do so, just the way that you could buy a Popsicle? Can you imagine the terror that must have gone through this frightened loving child's mind, the sheer terror that must have been going through his or her mother and his father's mind, can you? Who knows what happened to those mothers and fathers lives after that abduction from this master who they saw, but could do nothing about, or what happened to the lives of those children, those parents might have gone stark raving mad. Yes, they may have gone mad, being stolen, taken by White men as they watched, White men who could be playing some kind of sick mind game with them, or even worse some other kind of games with their bodies, and knowing that your son could be castrated, and your daughter raped, or both raped, being tortured, and possibly being made concubines for other sick White men and women is just too much to imagine. And after their use, even the possibility that they might even be tossed aside like garbage, or drowned like a rat, but this happened to some of these slaves. It should make one cringe to think of some child being snatched, but back in that time they didn't have to snatch the child, they could have just walked into the living quarters, and asked to see Jerome or Gerard, or Shirley or Malta and just tell the child to come, and the child had to go whether fighting, kicking and screaming or not, they had to go. Can you imagine your child being taken from you for fun and games by a master who didn't like the way a mother or father looked at them, or answered them, such terror? But that was terrorism.

These inept, slimy, ruthless dogs handled your children in

the worst ways that can be imagined, innocent children who really couldn't fight back, so they had to endure the pain and suffering from these White men and women who rendered them weak by sucking the life force from within them with their forceful torture and sick demented cruelty. Oh the White man has a lot to answer for, and in this country, and when they have the audacity to speak of terrorism, when you speak of terrorism, think, think back and look back at what you did to these wonderful people, look back and see how you terrorized them then and continued to terrorize them after slavery, for terrorism lasts.

You see Black people have been used to this kind of terror because it started with you White folks many many years ago, and that was real, it wasn't made up. Karma, it does come back, we all create our own karma, this country has created its own karma too, and can you imagine what it is that is coming back to this country? Oh the White man has much to answer for, he must not believe in a God, he can't, and to have the audacity to say that they're Christians, Christians, that's totally unimaginable. What kind of religion would allow them to do the things that they did, what religion would allow such a people to call themselves Christians after those acts that they perpetuated on other human beings? Tell me, and then tell me why they are still calling themselves Christians, because they still do.

As said before, to think that they actually read the same Bible that they used to teach the slaves with, enslaving their minds, it makes you wonder about this Bible, but as said earlier, God didn't write the Bible, man wrote the Bible, the White man wrote the Bible. The same White man who was screwing mothers and fathers and raping little boys and girls, whipping them with chains, burning them, tarring and feathering them, hanging them, and making sure that their people watched along with the onlookers who watched this terror. Terrorism, and this country wonders about terrorism in this country, the chicken must have come home to roost, but it must be coming again, for those thousands upon thousands upon thousands of families that this nation of a White people, a White-run government that terrorized the Black people, the African-American People of Color in and out of slavery.

Slavery was the epitome of terrorism, and the most violent terrorism that one could have imagined at that time. Poor White people, poor White trash with the nerve to steal our history, our children, and our dignity, having the balls to do all of that but not having the balls or gumption to admit that this was a cruel and unusual act, and that this was a crime against humanity. Think about this as you read and re-read if you must, and then try to imagine your sister, your brother or mother being raped, soiled by ignorant, arrogant, dirty low-class, no, that's no-class, White men and women. Think about it because it happened to us, the African-American People of Color, time and time again in slavery. And then after slavery was "ended", it still continued to happen because then they had more lynchings, they hung your ass, they were still able to spit in your face, still able to beat you, so where had slavery gone? They were still able to rape and sodomize you, so where had slavery gone? Blacks never won against Whites in this country's court of law, so where had slavery gone? Basically slavery was still here, they could call you by any name that they wanted to, and did, so where had slavery gone? They could steal from you, so where had slavery gone? And they could smack you, but you couldn't slap back because if you did, you could be arrested, beaten to death or hung. If you did go to jail after being arrested, there they had something special for the African-American People of Color, they had the chain gangs in prison, so Blacks were still in chains, still in chains, so tell me, tell me, America, where had slavery gone? You could still rob, rape and murder my people and get away with it, so where had slavery gone? And now, after all the sick, vile, and unspeakable terror that has been committed against us by you, it continues to have an effect on those that have been affected by these acts for a very long time, perhaps all of their lives because that's what happens in terrorism. Terrorism makes one fear, it makes one be afraid of things that were done, afraid of things that happened because if it was done once, who knows when something like that or something worse was going to happen to them? Truly, the White man has much to answer for.

You stole our children as if they were less than a loaf of bread, and to me that was one of most the frightening things that I ever saw portrayed in a movie. First off, can you imagine the fear that must have been in the minds of those African-American People of Color, the fear that the master would steal one of the children just because they showed too much affection? Imagine that just because they showed affection for their own children or fondness of a child that was theirs in the most loving way, which they should have been able to do for it was a blessing of the highest order, a blessing from God, a blessing that was not received every day. That fear, I remember now that's why their parents were afraid just to hug their children afterwards, all because of the stolen ones – terrorism.

The thought sends chills up and down my spine, and then the reality of having your child stolen from you by this White master totally blew my mind when I saw it, when it was acted, when it was portrayed on TV. But I quickly realized that this was real, that this had already happened, and only God knows how many times this happened. These are realities that this country does not want face up to or apologize for, but think about it, can you imagine your child being stolen by a master because he wanted to, because he could?

A Prayer for the Slaves That Have Gone Before

Oh Lord our God, we thank you for the Blessings that you have given us, and for all the slaves of the African-American People of Color who have gone before to make a way, so let their light so shine that we may know that their deaths were not in vain. Bless those children that were stolen too and for all the others who have died, Amen.

And I used to wonder for a very long time as I grew up why the African-Americans People of Color in this country, why so many of our families, didn't kiss and didn't hug one another. Why? Well, that was terrorism, that was the terror that was so imbedded in our parents' minds that it still had an effect on us, so it continued. They were still afraid, and they didn't know why they were afraid, but you see the terror from the White man, from slavery, still terrorized the African-American People of Color, and now this country is afraid, rather the White man is afraid of terrorism.

In a way that really seems kind of odd that they should be so afraid of terrorism, they had it their way for so long, look at their history, and how they terrorized people of color. They should have been afraid when they thought nothing of terrorizing little

Black boys and girls, and their mothers and fathers, that's when they should have been afraid. They should have been afraid when they were spitting in our faces, peeing on us, that's when they should have been afraid. They should have been afraid when they were hanging the African-American People of Color, that's when they should have been afraid. They should have been afraid when they were branding us like wild animals, that's when they should have been afraid. They should have been afraid when they were so busy burning down our churches, our homes and burning crosses on our lawns, that's when they should have been afraid. Or when they refused to let us drink from their White water fountains, or use their White bathrooms, that's when they should have been afraid. Or when they took those whips and beat us like wild beasts or shot us as if we were wild dogs attacking them, that's when they should have been afraid. They should have been afraid when they turned fire hoses on us, when they were busy stealing our children, that's when they should have been afraid. But to be afraid now, now after those planes crashed into the WTC, now after crashing into the Pentagon, and crashing into Pennsylvania, now because of 9/11 of 2001, they say that they are afraid, for terrorism has struck this so-called invincible country. Why be afraid now, why be afraid now when this incident, as grave as it was, as sick and deplorable as it was, is still not as sick and deplorable as what you did the African-American People of Color. And when it was just us that you were torturing and murdering, then you weren't afraid, you didn't even flinch as you continued to terrorize us, so you really shouldn't be afraid now either. These terrorists have nothing on you, they have done nothing compared to what you've done; your slavery still ranks too high on the list of all time acts of violence and crimes against humanity.

There is one big difference to what they did, they have taken credit and admitted that they are the terrorists, and they are not covering up what they did, and will continue to do so they say; they admit to their actions, unlike this country, unlike this United States of America, who will not admit to what they have done to the African-American People of Color, or apologize for doing so. It really is amazing, so now you say that you're afraid, well now it's a little too late for that, when you're not even sorry, so why should you be afraid now?

So you see that when you speak of terror to me now, it kind of rings deaf in my ears, for after all the terror that you've done to us, which still saturates the Black family, and you still refuse to apologize for things you've done, that's why I still cry, and I write. I write because of the terror, I write because of the torture, I write of the slavery, of the chains, the whips, the noose, and I write because of the fires that they set to our homes and churches and our businesses, that's why I write. I write because of all the immeasurable stolen moments, stolen visions, stolen blessings that will never come, for when you take the breath away from those that once breathed, it's gone forever. So I write, we write, for we must give voice to all our children's children, our grandmothers and grandfathers, our mothers and fathers, great-grandparents and great-great-grandparents. You stole the air that they once breathed because of your envious, sadomasochistic, evil, treacherous and vile ways.

There are reasons for our tears, but tears won't bring back the joy that could have been, the sisters that could have mothered or the brothers that could have fathered. No tears won't ever bring back that joy removed by you, for it was not accidental that you murdered and destroyed all that you had, look all around the world, for your violence precedes you, it's as though it's your calling card. This country is like the funny bone, you know when you hit that funny bone, it brings excruciating pain, it's no laughing matter, there's nothing "funny" about the funny bone, for it's not a laughing matter, just like this country, you're just like the funny bone, but you're not a laughing matter. Oh, there is a reason for writing, for the pain is that deep, if we kept writing to the end of time, the sorrow would still be there, for this was not an accident, all of what you've done has been done on purpose, and you continue.

i. America's Sick Humor

Speaking about something else that is really not a laughing matter is when people, comedians, try to make light of what is going on in Iraq. While watching one of the late night shows that I turned to for only a couple moments, something caught my ear that wasn't funny. The host was talking about the interim president of Iraq, and he said, "Well he's only interim until he's assassinated or killed," and the audience broke out in laughter, they laughed at that, that was sick, there's nothing funny about that.

What comedians get away with is really shameful, and even more shameful is America's sense of humor. Here we are in the 21st century, and this country is still very much involved in an extremely volatile situation in Iraq, a country that was invaded by this country, where many innocent civilians, men, women and children have been murdered, along with the soldiers that chose to fight in that war. A country that is still very much trying to overcome the obstacles that face them, and here in America, some late night host that makes millions of dollars each year is joking about an interim president, stating in joke mind you, that this interim president is only interim until he is assassinated or killed. Things that so many people find funny are really not laughable, not when you start joking about the most serious conditions that people and their nations face, especially after so much bloodshed has occurred and is still occurring, that's not only not funny, it's not even warped, it's sick.

However, one has to ask a question, does it reflect on the mindset of the people of this country when they will laugh at things that are utterly disgusting? You be the judge, and remember that there are other countries watching us, just as this country is watching them. Perhaps this is one reason why this country gets an "F" when it comes to taking care of its people. If the people continue to laugh at some of the jokes made by some of these late night hosts that are making millions of dollars each year, salaries much higher than most people will make in their lifetime, perhaps our government is saying, "Take care of whom, why these people laugh at sick humor, they're too busy watching and enjoying those late night shows, so we really don't have to worry about them." This government is probably looking at the situation this way saying: "Hum, how to care for our people, when people show us where their real concern lies, why they are probably even laughing at what is going on in Iraq, so we can continue with what we're doing, and we can give them what we want, and they'll take it, they don't demand our perfection, so they will never be any the wiser. Let them laugh and we'll laugh with them, we don't have to worry until they stop with their laughing and then, oh well, it will be too late."

14. Crimes the White Man Has to Answer for

Many are the crimes the White man and woman have to answer for, the so-called Black crimes of robbery, murder and rape that have been linked or pinned on the Black man, for so many of them have been falsely accused. Black people who were innocent, but because of some White person that gave a description of a Black man as being the assailant, pictures were drawn of this fictional man, causing this man, who was innocent, to be arrested. Some men were even convicted because those White people went as far as to give false testimony in a court of law, they perjured themselves, this was not only a false description, but because of a blatant lie.

This was not only a lie, it was also a betrayal. All the acts that have been committed against the AAPC throughout history are because of the duplicity which this country has been a part of throughout slavery, and the Civil Rights movement, so it would be wise to look at the betrayal of Whites to Blacks, and also the betrayal of this government to Blacks, when it comes to standing up for the truth. In these cases, it was Whites not standing up for Blacks when they knew that the crimes were committed by a White person and not the Black person, that's what's called saving their own White man's skin, but it is also betrayal.

Then you have the crimes that were committed against Black people who were murdered during the Civil Rights movement that still haven't been solved. No one ever came forward to tell what they saw, and as of today, those that are still alive still refuse come forward and tell the truth of what they witnessed. There is still a case that is fifty years old this year that still hasn't been solved, among others where those who know have kept their mouths closed, and these White people too are some of the people that call themselves Christians. Who do these people remind you of? Does it ring a bell about anything that has happened before? Well I will tell you, these people are just like this country, for this country still refuses to apologize to the AAPC and state that slavery was a cruel and unusual treatment, and that it was a crime against humanity, and they too call themselves Christians. This country is probably proud of them not coming forward and telling the truth, for they set the example. That's right, the United States of America has set the prime example, for it is the same kind of refusal that they have been involved in for over one hundred and thirty-five years.

If America can take their word for some of the things that the White man has supposedly seen and been a witness to, and then expose these lies on TV, publish them in newspapers and books, doesn't this make you wonder more and more about the credence of the Bible? Doesn't this tell you that this government must be complicit with those individuals and/or organizations that continue to perpetuate these things? You see this is not the start of the White man lying; this is something that he has been known to do, so why would anybody in his or her right mind believe him when it comes to something like the Bible? It does make a good story, in fact, it makes a great story, they call it the greatest story ever told, but one has to look at the source and really ask, can we believe this? He has always had a great imagination, he is great at fabrication, and even one of his own White brothers in another country had to ask, since when has the United States of America been know for telling the truth? America thinks that we're going to believe that they love and care for us now, when after all that has happened with our people being murdered, and those who murdered them not being brought to justice, when no one dares to come out to help solve a crime against the AAPC, or to open their mouth about a crime of injustice toward the AAPC, America think again.

Oh, I write because the joy was not there. I write because when I ride the bus, the subways, the trains and planes, and when I look at my beautiful Black men and women, I see the hurt, the pain, and the sorrow in our faces. I see the abuse for it too is still there, it's written in their faces, so just look at their faces sometimes and ask yourself, why are these beautiful people so sad and sullen? Ask yourself where the smile is, the glow that you think should be there, and try to answer. Perhaps you cannot see what I see, but it is there, and it is a sad sight indeed. There is pain written in these faces that is still hurtful to see; it's like looking at a loved one that you want to smile, but they cannot for they've lost a friend, perhaps in death or sudden accident, but you want to cheer them up but you cannot change that look of theirs. It is the same with my people as I watch them on the train, bus or plane. I write because of the stolen moments, I write because of the stolen joy, the sorrow and despair, I write so that I can get this out of the way, for this is not easy stuff to write. Oh, after this, how I look forward to writing about joy, joy that I know is forthcoming, it must because there has been too much sadness for us, too much sorrow and far too much pain and far too many tears, but this is something that my soul is telling me to write before I can write something else. This is like my prison, but soon I will free myself to fly out of this air that has weighed me down for so many years. Terrorism is a bitch and a bastard that the White man has raped all of the Black people with, so I must continue until this journey has come to an endearing enlightenment.

15. Black & White In This Country

Thinking about how things are in this country, especially when it comes to Black and White, this country itself has forced people to deal in colors, in themes of Black and White because of its discriminatory factor. Everybody in this country wasn't put on the same level through the constitution in the beginning, and this caused a lot of discrimination later throughout 20th century and also in the early 21st century, reason being that the structure made it so. Now, when people get angry because people say or ask why we have to say Black this and Black that, we ask, don't you remember? Since you seem to be prone to amnesia, we'll refresh your memory again. It is unfortunate that we have to do this, but this government made it so. You refused to acknowledge the works and so many accomplishments of the African-American People of Color, remember that you stole our history, you robbed us of things that we did so that it became necessary. And after all of the struggle that we've had with you to accomplish things that we have, it's just our time to put the nail in the coffin so to speak and to let ourselves shine so that you know it is us when we do something that is wonderful. So yes, it will continue to be Black this, Black that, for all of the things that you have denied us and still try to deny us today. America made it so that everything a Black person, African-American People of Color or person of color was trying to achieve or rise to, those things that had not been accomplished by a Black person before, this system's structure simply said no. Now after saying no for so long to Black people, pushing us aside as if we really didn't exist, i.e. ignoring us, you just can't expect or ask the African-American People of Color to drop our Blackness all because you say right now that we're "treating everyone the same".

As a people we have watched you, and we know that you're not to be trusted, so for us to believe you now would truly be a great mistake on our part, and we're too wise to take that bait. We know how you lie, and that equality part would be a lie, it's a falsehood, it's the same as the constitution, a falsehood, and the United States of America is still a falsehood too. They haven't proven to be as genuine and loving and respectful to the America they say they care about, and still by their actions they've shown that the African-American People of Color are still in another category, so one still has to ask, where do we fit in?

First off, we're still struggling to have elected officials of color in every major city where the African-American People of Color is a very sizable force, this is all because the country was formerly set up as Black and White, and it created discrimination that was designed to last. Divide and conquer, and it still is Black and White, divide and conquer, then divide and conquer again. Also, when you keep destroying our vote as was done in Florida, where the African-American People of Color weren't allowed to vote, and/or the vote was simply deleted, that's another reason for the Black vs. White, you are still doing wrong against us, that has not stopped, and this we know. You shouldn't even ask such an insipid question as why does it have to be Black this and Black that, why look across this country as your answers are written more than in the wind.

There are other great factors for this Blackness to be held in the spotlight: one, you keep it there when it comes to crimes, and two, the people of the United States are simply prejudice – White people, you're prejudiced, and Black people, you're prejudiced too. So in a prejudiced society, in a country in which you have 300 million Americans of which the Black population is still a minority compared to Whites, very much so, the higher rate for those discriminating would be that of White Americans. It's still a struggle for African-American People of Color to become as affluent as we'd like to. For instance, when it comes to buying homes and to electing officials, there are the White people who are still opposing Blacks by not voting for them just on the basis that they don't want a Black person in control, by not selling property to them, they don't want them in their neighborhood. Therefore, we must keep stressing our Blackness in each community across the United States of America, and in the media.

Then you have those things that come into prominence by the mere fact that crime sells newspapers. It's a media sensation, and they will run with it, and the stories that are highlighted in the big cities like New York City usually involve crime, and crime against the minorities, especially the Black communities, specifically the Black male, is featured, so just as it was in slavery, this is nothing new. It's all about how to demean a Black man. It really is amazing how this country and major cities react when a person of color, a Black man is involved; you don't have any problem in making this figure out to be the worst that one can imagine, that "how to" part you have mastered. That's a "how to" that American Whites have always known how to do, but how to tell the truth, how to care, how to love, that you have never found out how to do, or if you do, you just made like you didn't know how to care, or love, yet you pretend to teach these things this government has never shown in a classroom. How to destroy the young Black man – now this is something that you never had a problem with how to do. It goes back to slavery when you began castrating those beautiful African men because you were jealous of what you didn't have, and today you are still demeaning the Black man because he is still superior to you. There is also still a special kind of attraction, there's an aura that a Black man gives off, and still today your White women are mesmerized by this wonder of a man.

One case in particular of destroying the Black man is the case of Ahmed aka Amadou Diallo, a case where four police officers, all White, were found to have shot at this man of color forty-one times, hitting him nineteen times and then being acquitted of this crime.

http://en.wikipedia.org/wiki/Amadou_Diallo

Now to tell the mother, the father and family, and the world that he was acting suspiciously because they thought that he had a gun, this is absolutely absurd. This is an excuse that has been used for far too many times when White police officers are accused, and rightfully accused, of gunning down a person of color. Of course, they were wrong, unfortunately, that's all that's needed in this country when a person of color is confronted by White police officers. If you are a person of color, who knows, you could be praying, but if they say that you are acting suspiciously, then you are in trouble, they could possibly shoot you down. Can you imagine if the African-American People of Color or other people of color were like the Jews when they prayed, rocking back and forth at a wall? There would be more of us shot and/or killed. What if something like that happened to a person like me who is an epileptic, an epileptic who begins to act a little strange because he or she's trying to get to a position that they feel safe, or to hide, because there is a seizure coming on, what would they do after shooting that person?

It's the same as this Iraqi war, killing innocent people who did you no harm, and you shot them because you thought there were weapons of mass destruction there, but you were afraid, so this mistake was just unfortunate. However, you murdered those Iraqi people in cold blood because you could. Murdering because one can; it is about time that America stopped buying those false statements of said officers and started punishing these police officers for the crimes that they commit, and all of these law enforcement officers for the crimes that they do instead of letting them off, acquitting them because they say that they thought something that wasn't so.

They are always thinking something that for the most part wasn't true in the first place, and if this country hadn't designed you White folks to be so prejudiced, perhaps there would be more African-American People of Color and people of color alive today. One of these days, justice will come, and when it does, perhaps you'll be saying what the African-American People of Color have been saying all along, we are innocent people just going about our lives until you confronted us with your weapons of mass destruction.

Mistakes that cost lives aren't usually mistakes; they are usually done on purpose for there are just too many for the media to keep on calling mistakes. Here in New York City, and they talk about the south, well, we have extreme prejudice right here in this city – it's called trained prejudice. Forty-one times, nineteen shots that hit this man, a young man who had done no wrong, and no weapon was found. But they were acquitted because they, the defense, said that they thought that this innocent man had a weapon, but he did not, the only weapons were first those White police officers and second, the guns of the same White police officers. White men and weapons of mass destruction, that's exactly what they are, and then they had the case moved to upstate New York so that these White officers could get acquitted, and they did.

Another thing that continues to blow people's mind, especially the minds of African-American People of Color and other people of color, is when we are told by White people that this and other things of a similar nature are mistakes. Yet this predominately White system still wants the African-American People of Color and other people of color's support, and it still wants us to have respect for the weapons of mass destruction that walk our streets every day in the cities of this country – this is farcical.

We are a people needing to relax ourselves, oh, how we'd love to write more things, there is so much that is on our minds that we need to discuss as we write because this writing is not only all about sharing, it's about fulfilling ourselves as we write. Black people are the most important people right now, for as we share, we too must be fulfilled. Yes, Black people are the most important people here right now, we have to put ourselves as number one, we must because it's all about fulfilling, fulfilling our dreams that were snatched away by you.

Oh such beautiful people are we, we are wonderful people,

we are talented people, we are genius people, that's right genius, we are all geniuses because we carry in us a special blessing from above, and we are wonderful people because God created all of us, and while we nurtured you, He nurtured us. Oh we have nurtured so many of you White people in our lives, we spoke to you as strangers, even when in chains, some of you as friends, and even some of you became our lovers, husbands and wives. But now it's time, more than time, for our healing to begin within ourselves, and then for you, so we will write, so we think, so we will write, and we will speak, so we write, and we will touch as we write, and we will hear as we write, and we will listen as we write, so we write, and we'll feel what we write, and we'll hold ourselves as we write, and we will write. Then we will do as you have done, for as you have hugged, we will begin to hug and hold, then we will write, and then we'll smile, so we write as we hear, and we will see and we will touch, and we will feel, then we will hear those sounds, and then we'll write.

Our feelings of emotion that we have and have had all through our lives, and you know this for you've seen it, and sometimes you have laughed as we cried, but we've shared it with you just the same, but now we will write and we will nurture, and we will nurture ourselves, and then we'll write and we'll see and nurture us some more, but that main people that we'll keep nurturing is ourselves, and we'll continue to write, and we will write and feel, we will see and we'll hear, we'll touch, then we'll feel and we'll sense and then we'll hug, and we'll smile and we'll laugh, then we'll write as we cry, for those tears that we make, this time will be tears of joy, and we'll smile, and we'll laugh some more, and then we'll tickle, and we'll smile, and then we'll write, oh so much love that we will write, and so much love that we'll speak, so much love that we feel, and with this love that we write, and that we'll share with our writing, and we'll continue to write, and we'll continue to speak, and we'll write, and we will breath as we write, and we will smell as we write, we'll taste as we write, and we'll sense, and in our sensing we'll hear, and we'll touch as we write, so in all these things that we have seen, we will write with a love that we feel, that's why we will continue to write, and we'll continue to write what and as we feel, so we'll write, and we'll write, and we'll love as we write of those cherished moments that we saved just to nurture ourselves from when we once cried, so we'll write, and we'll write and we'll write.

I Light This Candle

I light this candle for all the slaves that have gone before us,
for those which have suffered so much pain, more pain than of
joy,
from a government so cruel, that chose a people like us,
to whip and to chain makes no sense to me,
but I light this candle for the unspeakable ones
that once tortured you, and for the unspeakable crimes
that have tormented you too, and as I light this candle
I light it out of love and for so much respect
that I have for our people like you, for our people that
have been scarred in such unbelievable ways,
that to me that would seem such an insufferable thought,
I light this candle for your children too for the innocence
that they had, until they were taken from you,
an idea so obscene that it must have been too hard to have seen,

so I light this candle for the hearts that have cried,
for the tears that have streamed
and for those that once screamed,
for the sorrow not the joy, and for the grief that you bared,
I light this candle for that which was stolen from you,
and ask at this time may God grant you peace,
and hope that this light may help to enlighten our world,
for I light this candle so that others may see,
that the cruelty of man need not continue to be,
today is a light, as every light should be,
so bright filled with hope for others to see,
so I light this candle for the joy to be,
as the birds have sung, may you sing joy too,
as I light this candle for you on this wonderful morn,
peace and love be God's Blessing to you,
for you have shown me the strength to love, Amen

04/26/2005

Addendum
Born In The Wrong Country

Reference to P. 16

Website figures as of November 07, 2008

http://zfacts.com/p/447.html

Money spent to date on the Iraqi war 2008

Cost of Iraq War 2008

Graph shows budget authority for **Iraq war** in each fiscal year (ending Sept. 30). Think how it would be if some other planet invaded the U.S. and **spent**

$588 billion dollars plus.

The cost continues rising daily, moment by moment.

Before the war, White House economic adviser Lawrence Lindsay estimated the cost at $100 to $200 billion. So the White House got rid of him and "re-estimated" the cost at $50 to $60 billion. It's now over $500 billion.

http://www.sfgate.com/cgi-bin/article.cgi?f=/c/a/2008/06/19/MN9211C17R.DTL

$162 billion

House approves $162 billion war-spending bill

Zachary Coile, Chronicle Washington Bureau

Friday, June 20, 2008

http://theiraqinsider.blogspot.com/2008/02/how-much-does-iraq-war-cost-per-month.html

Website figures as of November 07, 2008

How much does Iraq war cost per month, week, day, hour, minute, second?

Reference: to page 41-43

http://icasualties.org/oif/.

http://www.iraqbodycount.net/.

These websites are still active, but the numbers show how much these figures have changed since 2005, showing how much more death and destruction has occurred since that time.

http://icasualties.org/oif/

U.S. Confirmed Deaths

Reported Deaths: 4192

Confirmed Deaths: 4190

Pending Confirmation: 2

DoD Confirmation List as of 11/07/2008 – DoD stands for Department of Defense

As of 11/07/2008

http://www.iraqbodycount.net/

88,878 – 97,005 from 2003-2008

As searched in January 2007, and as of 2006 from different websites within the search of:

http://www.google.com/custom?q=Amount+of+money+that+has +been+spent+on+the+Iraqi+war&sa=Search+TO+Archives&cof =S%3Ahttp%3A%2F%2Fwww.truthout.org%3BGL%3A0%3B

AH%3Acenter%3BLH%3A45%3BL%3Ahttp%3A%2F%2Fww
w.truthout.org%2Fimgs.site_01%2F1.LGO.search_1.gif%3BLW
%3A455%3BAWFID%3A3525fa9668c9622d%3B&domains=w
ww.truthout.org&sitesearch=

http://www.tompaine.com/articles/2006/09/28/the_opportunity_c
ost_of_war.php gives the amount spent of the Iraqi war as $320
billion.

http://www.thewashingtonnote.com/archives/001546.php.   The
cost has now gone beyond $432 billion.   Other sites from the
same Google website say that the cost could rise beyond 2
trillion dollars.

http://www.guardian.co.uk/Iraq/Story/0,2763,1681119,00.html

Reference: P. 132

http://www.nationalpriorities.org/costofwar_home

http://www.washingtonpost.com/wp-
dyn/content/article/2008/03/07/AR2008030702846_pf.html

http://www.antiwar.com/casualties/

U.S. military deaths in Iraq war at 4,191 – **As of 11/07/2008**

Reference: P. 49

http://query.nytimes.com/gst/fullpage.html?res=9906E0DF173A
F934A35751C1A96E958260

Reference: P. 51

http://husseini.org/2007/01/martin-luther-king-jr-why-i-am.html

http://lib.berkeley.edu/MRC/pacificaviet/riversidetranscript.html

Reference: P.52

Bread Lines on *Sixty Minutes* twice on CBS in 2004

I've been boiling inside ever since watching tonight's sixty minutes, detailing the wait in line for basic foodstuffs by more than a thousand working-class Western Ohioans.

http://www.democraticunderground.com/discuss/duboard.php?a z=view_all&address=105x138934

http://www.cbsnews.com/stories/2003/01/08/60II/main535732.s html

Reference: P. 95

http://www.hippy.com/php/article-114.html

You tell me in that history book of yours that you came to these shores and DISCOVERED a country that was already occupied...

http://www.hippy.com/php/article-114.html

Reference: P. 113

They are closing VA hospitals, yet Congress and the Senate appropriated $87 billion dollars to fight this invasion – http://www.sfgate.com/cgi-bin/article.cgi?file=/chronicle/archive/2003/09/08/MN21238.DT L

http://sadparade.typepad.com/sad_parade/iraq_regress_report/,

This is an updated website which tells of the closing of the VA hospitals and VA hospitals that have been closed.

http://maloney.house.gov/index.php?Itemid=61&id=995&option =com_content&task=view

http://www.usatoday.com/news/washington/2004-05-06-va-system_x.htm

http://sadparade.typepad.com/sad_parade/iraq_regress_report
The above website no longer exists. Another website which gives the amount of spent on the Iraq war is:

http://www.ourfuture.org/makingsense/factsheet/iraq-war-costs.

Reference: P. 115

As searched in January 2007, and as of 2006 from these different websites within the search of:

http://www.google.com/custom?q=Amount+of+money+that+has +been+spent+on+the+Iraqi+war&sa=Search+TO+Archives&cof =S%3Ahttp%3A%2F%2Fwww.truthout.org%3BGL%3A0%3B AH%3Acenter%3BLH%3A45%3BL%3Ahttp%3A%2F%2Fww w.truthout.org%2Fimgs.site_01%2F1.LGO.search_1.gif%3BLW %3A455%3BAWFID%3A3525fa9668c9622d%3B&domains=w ww.truthout.org&sitesearch=

http://www.tompaine.com/articles/2006/09/28/the_opportunity_c ost_of_war.php

http://www.thewashingtonnote.com/archives/001546.php.
http://www.guardian.co.uk/Iraq/Story/0,2763,1681119,00.html

Reference: P. 116

http://mindprod.com/politics/iraq.html

Reference: P. 178

10,667 cases of sexual abuse from 1950 through 2002 in the Catholic Church alone, and over $840,000,000.00 have been paid out since the 1950's.

http://www.betnahrain.org/bbs/index.pl/noframes/read/23525

http://www.democraticunderground.com/discuss/duboard.php?a
z=view_all&address=104x3144928

Edited on Sat Feb-19-05 07:59 PM by Dookus by the American
Catholic Church.

http://formercatholicsforchrist.yuku.com/topic/3788

A 2004 report by the U.S. Catholic Church said that 10,667
people have accused 4,392 priests with sexual abuse. Costs to
settle cases currently exceed $1.5 billion, with thousands of
cases yet pending.

Catholic authorities have largely succeeded in labeling the
offending priests as pedophiles. However, most of the victims
have not been young children, but boys in their mid to late teens.

http://www.usmessageboard.com/religion-and-ethics/25121-
catholic-church-demands-celibacy-for-gays-too.html

Underpinning concerns among U.S. Church leaders and
conservative Catholics is a 2004 survey by John Jay College of
criminal justice that found that of 10,667 individuals abused by
priests between 1950 and 2002, 81% were male.

http://books.google.com/books?ct=result&q=Catholic+Church,+
$840,000,000&btnG=Search+Books,

Reference: P. 210

One case in particular of destroying the Black man is the case of
Ahmed (aka Amadou) Diallo, a case where four police officers, all
White, were found to have shot at this man of color forty-one times,
hitting him nineteen times and then being acquitted of this crime.

http://en.wikipedia.org/wiki/Amadou_Diallo

* 9 7 8 0 5 7 8 0 0 0 4 8 0 *